# The Tyndale Old Testament Commentaries

*General Editor:*
PROFESSOR D. J. WISEMAN, O.B.E., M.A., D.Lit., F.B.A.,
F.S.A.

# ESTHER

D0618696

# ESTHER

## AN INTRODUCTION AND COMMENTARY

by

### JOYCE G. BALDWIN, B.A., B.D.
*formerly Dean of Women, Trinity College, Bristol*

INTER-VARSITY PRESS
LEICESTER, ENGLAND
DOWNERS GROVE, ILLINOIS, U.S.A.

**Inter-Varsity Press**
*38 De Montfort Street, Leicester LE1 7GP, England*
*P.O. Box 1400, Downers Grove, Illinois 60515, U.S.A.*
*© Joyce G. Baldwin 1984*

*Inter-Varsity Press, England, is the publishing division of the Universities and Colleges Christian Fellowship (formerly Inter-Varsity Fellowship), a student movement linking Christian Unions in universities and colleges throughout the United Kingdom and the Republic of Ireland, and a member movement of the International Fellowship of Evangelical Students. For information about local and national activities write to UCCF, 38 De Montfort Street, Leicester LE1 7GP.*

*InterVarsity Press, U.S.A., is the book-publishing division of Inter-Varsity Christian Fellowship, a student movement active on campus at hundreds of universities, colleges and schools of nursing. For information about local and regional activities, write IVCF, 233 Langdon Street, Madison, WI 53703.*

*Excerpts from* The Jerusalem Bible, *copyright © 1966 by Darton, Longman & Todd Ltd. and Doubleday & Company, Inc. Reprinted by permission of the publisher.*

*Text set in 10/10 Baskerville*
*Phototypeset by Input Typesetting Ltd., London*
*Printed in the United States of America*

---

**British Library Cataloguing in Publication Data**

*Baldwin, Joyce G.*
  *Esther—(The Tyndale Old Testament commentaries)*
  *1. Bible. (O.T. Esther—Commentaries)*
  *I. Title  II. Bible. O.T. Esther. English*
  *III. Series*
  *222'.907        BS1375.3*

*UK ISBN 0-85111-639-6 (hardback)*
*UK ISBN 0-85111-840-2 (paperback)*

---

**Library of Congress Cataloging in Publication Data**

*Baldwin, Joyce G.*
  *Esther: an introduction and commentary.*

  *(The Tyndale Old Testament commentaries; 12)*
  *1. Bible.  O.T.  Esther—Commentaries.  I. Title.*
*II. Series.*
*BS1375.3.B35        1984        222'.907        84-15670*
*USA ISBN 0-87784-964-1 (hardback)*
*USA ISBN 0-87784-262-0 (paperback)*
*USA ISBN 0-87784-880-7 (set of Tyndale Old Testament Commentaries, hardback)*
*USA ISBN 0-87784-280-9 (set of Tyndale Old Testament Commentaries, paperback)*

---

*16    15    14    13    12    11    10*
*97*

# GENERAL PREFACE

THE aim of this series of *Tyndale Old Testament Commentaries*, as it was in the companion volumes on the New Testament, is to provide the student of the Bible with a handy, up-to-date commentary on each book, with the primary emphasis on exegesis. Major critical questions are discussed in the introductions and additional notes, while undue technicalities have been avoided.

In this series individual authors are, of course, free to make their own distinct contributions and express their own point of view on all debated issues. Within the necessary limits of space they frequently draw attention to interpretations which they themselves do not hold but which represent the stated conclusions of sincere fellow Christians.

The book of Esther is a unique and vivid story of the struggles of a minority people and faith. Nevertheless many still criticize it for the absence of the Divine Name and for aspects of nationalism and vindictiveness it portrays. The author faces these and other matters squarely and sees God at work in national and personal affairs. The result is another sensitive commentary, full of carefully researched details illuminating the historical and cultural background, which emphasizes the spiritual and literary value of the book. Joyce Baldwin also gives us many insights and draws out the lessons applicable to any turbulent time.

In the Old Testament in particular no single English translation is adequate to reflect the original text. The authors of these commentaries freely quote various versions, therefore, or give their own translation, in the endeavour to make the more difficult passages or words meaningful today. Where necessary, words from the Hebrew (or Aramaic) Text underlying their studies are transliterated. This will help the reader who may be unfamiliar with the Semitic languages to identify the word under discussion and thus to follow the argument. It is assumed throughout that the reader will have ready access to one, or more, reliable rendering of the Bible in English.

Interest in the meaning and message of the Old Testament continues undiminished and it is hoped that this series will thus further the systematic study of the revelation of God and his will and ways as seen in these records. It is the prayer of the editor and publisher, as of the authors, that these books will help many to understand, and to respond to, the Word of God today.

D. J. WISEMAN

# CONTENTS

## AUTHOR'S PREFACE

IT was in the late 1960s that I first began to put my mind to the book of Esther, having been invited to contribute on Ruth and Esther to *The New Bible Commentary Revised*. I have never enquired whether it was a coincidence that these two books bearing women's names were allocated to the only woman contributor. Certainly I was well pleased to research these rewarding books, for which I have had a special love ever since, and I am grateful to the Editor of the Tyndale series for inviting me to write this commentary.

The footnotes reveal that I have been indebted to many people in the course of getting to grips with many fascinating aspects of this book of Esther. In particular I should like to acknowledge my debt to Trinity College, Bristol, for permitting me to make use of the library, now that I no longer do so by right.

In general I have used the RSV text of the Bible, and quotations are from that version unless otherwise indicated.

JOYCE BALDWIN

# CHIEF ABBREVIATIONS

| | |
|---|---|
| *AB* | *The Anchor Bible: Esther* by Carey A. Moore, 1979. |
| *AJSLL* | *American Journal of Semitic Languages and Literature.* |
| *ANET* | *Ancient Near Eastern Texts Relating to the Old Testament* by J. B. Pritchard, $^2$ 1955, ($^3$ 1969). |
| *ATD* | *Das Alte Testament Deutsch.* |
| AV | English Authorized Version (King James), 1611. |
| *BA* | *The Biblical Archaeologist.* |
| BDB | *Hebrew-English Lexicon of the Old Testament* by F. Brown, S. R. Driver and C. A. Briggs, 1907. |
| Berg | *The Book of Esther* by Sandra Beth Berg, 1979. |
| *CB* | *The Cambridge Bible: Esther* by A. W. Streane, 1907. |
| *CBQ* | *Catholic Biblical Quarterly.* |
| *CeB* | *The Century Bible* (New Series): *Ezra, Nehemiah and Esther* by L. H. Brockington, 1969. |
| *DNTT* | *The New International Dictionary of New Testament Theology* edited by Colin Brown. Vol. 1, 1975; Vol. 2, 1976; Vol. 3, 1978. |
| *EB* | *The Expositor's Bible: Esther* by W. F. Adeney, 1893. |
| EVV | English Versions. |
| GNB | Good News Bible: Today's English Version, 1976. |
| Heb. | Hebrew. |
| *HPE* | *History of the Persian Empire* by A. T. Olmstead, 1948. |
| *HUCA* | *Hebrew Union College Annual.* |
| *IB* | *The Interpreter's Bible*: Vol. III, *Esther* by B. W. Anderson, 1954. |
| *IBD* | *The Illustrated Bible Dictionary.* 3 vols., 1980. |
| *ICC* | *International Critical Commentary*: *Esther* by L. B. Paton, 1908. |

| | |
|---|---|
| *IDB* | *The Interpreter's Dictionary of the Bible.* 4 vols., 1962. |
| *IOT* | *Introduction to the Old Testament* by R. K. Harrison, 1970. |
| JB | The Jerusalem Bible, Standard Edition, 1966. |
| *JBL* | *Journal of Biblical Literature.* |
| *JNES* | *Journal of Near Eastern Studies.* |
| *JSOT* | *Journal for the Study of the Old Testament.* |
| *LB* | *Linguistica Biblica.* |
| *LOT* | *Introduction to the Literature of the Old Testament* by S. R. Driver, [8] 1909. |
| LXX | The Septuagint (pre-Christian Greek version of the Old Testament). |
| mg. | margin. |
| MS | manuscript. |
| MT | Massoretic Text. |
| *NBC* | *New Bible Commentary* (Third Edition) edited by D. Guthrie, J. A. Motyer, A. M. Stibbs and D. J. Wiseman, 1970. |
| NEB | The New English Bible: Old Testament, 1970. |
| NIV | New International Version, 1978. |
| *NPOT* | *New Perspectives on the Old Testament* edited by J. Barton Payne, 1970. |
| *OTA* | *Old Testament Abstracts.* |
| *PCB* | *Peake's Commentary on the Bible* (Revised Edition) edited by M. Black and H. H. Rowley, 1962. |
| *PIOT* | *Introduction to the Old Testament* by Robert H. Pfeiffer, British Edition, 1952. |
| RSV | American Revised Standard Version, 1952. |
| RV | English Revised Version, 1881. |
| SBL | Society of Biblical Literature. |
| *SEÅ* | *Svensk Exegetisk Årsbok.* |
| *TB* | *Tyndale Bulletin.* |
| *TBC* | *Torch Bible Commentary: Esther* by G. A. F. Knight, 1955. |
| *TOTC* | *Tyndale Old Testament Commentary.* |
| *VT* | *Vetus Testamentum.* |
| *VTS* | *Vetus Testamentum Supplement.* |
| *ZAW* | *Zeitschrift für die Alttestamentliche Wissenschaft.* |

# INTRODUCTION

**E**VERYONE loves a story. If it tells of one's own ancestors, shows them in a good light, and gives evidence of
a divine providence working to secure their survival, all
the more strongly does it appeal. All these conditions are
fulfilled in the book of Esther. Though no mention is made of
God's providence, it nevertheless plays a prominent part, and
may even give the book its *raison d'être*. The dramatic reversal
of a disastrous fate that had seemed set to wipe out the whole
Jewish race so impressed the writer that he applied himself
with all his artistic powers to conveying the events in writing,
and his account so fascinated Jewish readers that the book
became a best seller and went into many languages and
variant editions. It continues to be the number one favourite
with Jewish communities, and is read in the family every year
at Purim, as has been the traditional custom through the
centuries. Christians, by contrast, have not known quite what
to make of this book. By its very nature it raises for both
Jewish and Christian interpreters questions as to the part
played by narrative in Scripture. Laws and prophetic
warnings seem easier to interpret because they give express
commands to be obeyed, but a story may contain no such
directive. The initial purpose of a story, after all, is to captivate
and hold the interest of the listeners.

### I. THE PLACE OF NARRATIVE IN SCRIPTURE

The many parables used by Jesus in his teaching ought to
alert us to the many advantages of story-telling over more
academic styles of conveying truth. The Bible is meant for
ordinary people, who do not find abstract thought, and
especially theological concepts, absorbing. They do, however,
enjoy a story, and readily identify with its characters and their
dilemmas, and want to know how it all ends. The young
Hudson Taylor, off duty and bored, picked up a tract for want

13

of anything better to read. Intending to switch off before he got to the moral, he found himself involved and mastered by its message.[1] In just such a way the stories of the Bible catch us off guard and penetrate our defences. Having once captured our imagination, a story can 'take off' and, like a seedling transplanted into receptive soil, begin a life of its own in the reader's mind. The figurative language underlines the need to absorb the story into one's mind and not just to listen superficially, for its significance lies deeper than surface level.

One of the outstanding marks of biblical narrative is its lifelike quality of character and action. 'The biblical writers fashion their personages with a complicated, sometimes alluring, often fiercely insistent individuality because it is in the stubbornness of human individuality that each man and woman encounters God or ignores Him, responds to or resists Him.'[2] Not that character is fully delineated, for usually the text is tantalizingly concise and selective. Nevertheless the very selectivity highlights purpose. These biblical writers knew human nature but they also knew their God, and therefore they had an urgent reason for writing.

It may not be out of place to digress for a moment in order to consider secular narrative writing and what it may achieve. The serious novelist, sensitive to the world's problems, probing them in order to diagnose what is going on, is well placed to make others aware of the truths he has seen. William Golding, for example, in *Lord of the Flies* most movingly presents unpalatable truths about human nature. The same concepts, expressed in dogmatic form, provoke objections and stubborn resistance, whereas the schoolboys who become self-appointed leaders are agonizingly familiar. When in the end 'Ralph wept for the end of innocence . . . the darkness of man's heart, and the fall through the air of the true, wise friend called Piggy', the reader weeps with him. Whatever may have been the intention of the author, he leaves the reader under no illusion as to the fallenness of human nature. So desperate, indeed, does he show our human plight to be that the reader is left longing for some way out of the hopelessness, but it is not part of Golding's intention in this novel to point to a

[1]A. J. Broomhall, *Hudson Taylor and China's Open Century.* I: *Barbarians at the Gates* (Hodder and Stoughton and Overseas Missionary Fellowship, 1981), pp. 350–352.

[2]Robert Alter, *The Art of Biblical Narrative* (George Allen and Unwin, 1981), p. 189.

14

remedy. It is important, however, to see that this novelist achieves something which the preacher does not easily achieve, namely conviction of sin as the great fact of humanity. The story has succeeded where the plain statement, though greeted with assent, may fail to convince.

This truth is put in academic terms by James G. Williams: 'Biblical narrative represents a dynamic mode of thinking whose aesthetic properties support and enhance the process of arriving at knowledge.'[1] In other words stories make for easier learning. Presented with artistry and skill they enable us to enter into other people's lives and to learn from their experience, provided that the life-setting depicted is sufficiently similar to that of the listeners for there to be identification of interests. In that case a smile of recognition or, conversely, a gasp followed by an angry reaction indicates that deep down the story has found its mark. Nathan's parable is a case in point; the prophet can turn the tables on David and say 'You are the man' (2 Sa. 12:7).

Unquestionably, then, parables can be very effective in bringing home to the conscience a wrong committed but glossed over.

The book of Esther, however, is not a parable. Rather it relates an incident that has many marks of historicity, though certain aspects of the story have often been considered unlikely to have happened in real life. The author has also been accused of exaggerating some details. In order to appreciate his book we need to understand his purpose in writing, and, if possible, to discover whether he was relating an incident that actually happened, much as an inhabitant of the British Isles in 1940 might tell the story of the Battle of Britain, impressed by the extraordinary deliverance that had taken place. The literary style need not be that of the history book. Inevitably certain features will stand out in importance for the writer, who will be as selective as his medium demands. Literary aspects are therefore important in arriving at the mind of the author. As Martin Luther wrote: 'I am persuaded that without skill in literature, genuine theology cannot stand . . . The remarkable disclosure of the Word of God would never have taken place had he not first prepared the way by

[1] J. G. Williams, *Women Recounted: Narrative Thinking and the God of Israel* (Almond Press, Sheffield, 1982), p. 15.

rediscovery of languages and sciences.'[1] Ideally there needs also to be rediscovery of literature belonging to the area and period from which our book comes, and the ability to read and assess it, for the literary models of Western Europe are hardly likely to be the best guide to a book from Asia in the centuries before Christ. That some are available is a matter for thanksgiving, though it also requires adventure into unfamiliar territory. Archaeology also has its contribution to make to the background scene.

In short, a commentary requires us, with the help of many others who have recorded their studies, to look at the book from many points of view. In the last analysis, however, having assessed what it was saying to the original readers and listeners in the scattered Jewish communities of the centuries before Christ, it will be necessary to ask what response the book demands of the church and of the individual Christian today. Since the book is in Scripture it demands a verdict.

## II. THE BOOK'S HISTORICAL ACCURACY

Whatever literary genre an author adopts for his work, whether poetry, drama, short story or novel, if he chooses a theme from history he knows he has to accept as unchangeable the basic events. He can have some latitude where motivation is concerned, but the writer of Esther does not develop this theme. Like his modern counterparts he has had to face his critics on the thoroughness of his research and on his use of the accepted historical data. To look at the historical accuracy of his work is legitimate and necessary, and does not prejudge the question of literary genre.

There are, however, several marks of history writing in the way the book of Esther is narrated, such as the opening phrase of the Hebrew, *wayᵉhi* 'Now it came to pass' (AV, RV). Details of the time and place of the action follow: the name of the reigning monarch, the extent of his empire and the year of his reign at the commencement of the story. To this other circumstantial details are added as the plot develops, and at the end the reader is referred to a source book for verification and further study (10:2). So the author presents his work as if it were history, though this is the kind of information we

[1] In his letter to Eoban Hess, 29 March 1523. Quoted by A. C. Thiselton, 'Understanding God's Word Today', in John Stott (ed.), *Obeying Christ in a Changing World* (Collins Fountain Books, 1977), p. 99.

should expect him to include even if he were composing a historical novel.

*a. The Persian monarchy*

The events of the book took place, so the writer tells us (1:1) in the reign of King Ahasuerus (486–465 BC), who is better known by his Greek name Xerxes.[1] He was the son and successor of Darius I Hystaspes, at the beginning of whose reign the restoration of the Jerusalem Temple took place (Hg. 2:1–9; Zc. 7:1; 8:9). It was completed in 516 BC. The decree of Cyrus had permitted the return of captives from Babylon to Jerusalem in 539, at the very beginning of the Persian period. Comparatively few had availed themselves of the opportunity either then or on later occasions, and sixty years later large numbers of Jews remained in the eastern half of the Persian empire, many in the great imperial cities of Persia itself. Very little is known about them, apart from the evidence provided by the book of Esther, and the brief reference to the reign of Ahasuerus in Ezra 4:6, which provides independent evidence of opposition to Jewish interests. But despite hostility there were Jews who rose to positions of influence, as Daniel had done during the previous century at the court of Nebuchadrezzar (Dn. 2:48). There was something altogether fitting about the rise to power in an alien culture of those who honoured the one true God, even though they suffered as a consequence of their loyalty to him. In the book of Esther a new element is introduced to the theme of suffering. The Jews were victimized because they kept themselves to themselves, observing their own laws and customs (3:8). From this it was easy to accuse them of disregarding the laws of the Persian state, whether the accusation were true or not. There is no reason to doubt that, then as now, such victimization was a fact of experience (*cf.* Lv. 19:33–34).

In this connection, however, attention has been drawn to the benevolence of Persian rulers, and on this ground it has been thought unlikely that Ahasuerus would have countenanced Haman's suggestion to destroy a whole section of the population (3:9). Carey A. Moore, for example, expresses a need for more specific epigraphic material to attest to the existence of pogroms against the Jews 'in an otherwise tolerant

---

[1] The Greek versions identify the Persian king as Artaxerxes, and other kings were also suggested, but, in the light of evidence from the monuments, there is now general agreement that Ahasuerus/Xerxes is intended.

ESTHER

Achaemenian empire'.[1] Though there is no reason to doubt the generally accepted view of Cyrus the Great, the founder of the Achaemenian dynasty, as a wise and benevolent ruler, it has recently been pointed out that the evidence from the Cyrus Cylinder should be seen to be a standardized eulogy. It is a typical Mesopotamian building text, in which the ruler is always depicted as 'good'.[2] The purpose of the text was to commend the ruler to the god whose temple was being restored, in this case Marduk of Babylon, and to the conquered people as a faithful upholder of revered traditions. The idea that the successors of Cyrus were as humane and benevolent as he was, has been shown by Amelie Kuhrt to have been naive. She points out that tolerant policies were soon reversed when any subversive activity was suspected. 'Note the destruction of Babylon . . . by Xerxes after revolts in Babylonia in the early part of his reign.'[3] She also lists examples proving that the Achaemenids practised deportation of populations as part of their policy, just as the Assyrians and Babylonians had done. This correction of a widespread misapprehension helps to set King Ahasuerus in a realistic historical light. He was not above using the very same policies as had been followed by the much criticized Assyrians, and would have had no scruples in issuing the edicts of the book of Esther.

The same impression results from a reading of *The Histories* of Herodotus, one third of which is devoted to the reign of Xerxes [Ahasuerus]. Herodotus shows Xerxes in action in all sorts of circumstances connected with the invasion of Greece. Xerxes comes across as ambitious, and a bold warrior with vision and confidence, once he has overcome superstitious fears, and weighed to his own satisfaction contradictory advice. He is not averse to asking for the opinion of others, including that of Artemisia, a woman officer in his army who is given special mention by Herodotus, before and after the battle of Salamis.[4] According to the historian he found her advice most agreeable. There is plenty of evidence for his

[1]'Archaeology and the Book of Esther', *BA* 38 (1975), p. 180.
[2]Amelie Kuhrt, 'The Cyrus Cylinder and Achaemenid Imperial Policy', *JSOT* 25 (1983), pp. 83, 88. For a colour photograph of this famous inscription see *IBD* I, p. 353.
[3]*Art. cit.*, p. 94. In a footnote Kuhrt adds, 'The changed status of Babylon in relation to the Achaemenids after this is reflected in the fact that no Persian king after Xerxes' fourth regnal year bears the title "King of Babylon".'
[4]*The Histories* vii. 99; viii. 97, 104.

exploits with women, and of his intention to have his own way, even with his brother's wife and daughter. The mutilation and murder that followed this incident show the disgraceful lengths to which the king would go, and demonstrate that the dismissal of one queen and the choice of another, from whatever background, was quite within the bounds of the probable, even though in theory he was committed by his father's youthful agreement that the king should marry within seven noble families.[1] Though Herodotus is writing from the perspective of a Greek observer, the world he shows us is recognizably that of the book of Esther.

To possess a work of history, written in the very century when the events of the book of Esther took place (for Herodotus was born between 490 and 480 BC), is a remarkable providence. It supplies an example of history-writing contemporary with the period covered by Esther, by which to assess its contents. The translator of *The Histories* reminds us that they were written for public recitation at private gatherings or public festivals,[2] and we may assume that the same was true for Esther. In addition to the writing of Herodotus, Persian inscriptions of the fifth century BC add their witness, while thousands of tablets from Persepolis have greatly increased knowledge of world history, and more specifically of Persia. 'From these sources we have confirmation of what Herodotus says about Persian administration, but now we can describe the system in minute detail and with numerous illustrations.'[3] Though Herodotus was remarkably impartial and tolerant, it is a great gain to be able to listen to orientals relating events from their point of view. The reliefs at Persepolis even depict Ahasuerus as crown prince, standing behind the throne of his father Darius.[4] Though there is not much attempt at portraiture, in one way and another it is possible to get to know this Persian monarch of the book of Esther. That all the information about him dovetails so well supports the general accuracy of the source material, including the biblical book.

[1] *The Histories* xx. 108–111; iii. 84. In connection with Darius's marriage J. S. Wright shows that Xerxes' mother was not from one of the approved families (*NPOT*, p. 88).
[2] Aubrey de Selincourt, translator and writer of the Introduction to the Penguin Edition, 1954.
[3] A. T. Olmstead, *History of the Persian Empire* (University of Chicago Press, 1948), p. xiv.
[4] See, *e.g.*, *IBD* I, p. 24. Xerxes was responsible for the most polished of these reliefs.

According to Esther the court of Ahasuerus was situated at Susa (AV Shushan), the ancient capital of Elam where Darius had resided and built a palace complex that seemed to him unusually beautiful.[1] The first task of the new king was to complete what his father had begun in Susa, and two inscriptions testify to his residence there early in his reign.[2] The lavish entertainment, the abundance of gold and the glorious colours of the curtains and marble described in the first chapter are completely corroborated elsewhere. In the foundation deposit of Darius himself, discovered during excavations at Susa, exotic building materials are listed.[3] These were imported from all over the empire, including Ethiopia and India which are named together as the source of ivory (*cf.* Est. 1:1). The early excavations at Susa by M. A. Dieulafoy lacked the scientific precision achieved today, and had to contend with a confusion of ruins, looted already by Alexander the Great and his successors. Nevertheless the main features of the palace complex have been identified. These include the throne room, the harem and the position of the paradise or garden, watered by the nearby river (*cf.* Est. 1:5; 7:7). If the author of Esther did not know Susa at first hand he was extremely well informed about the royal residence, as well as about the character of the king.

### b. The names Esther and Mordecai

One of the strongest arguments against the historicity of the book rests on the evidence of Herodotus that Xerxes' queen during the relevant period was called Amestris.[4] Various arguments have been used in an attempt to account for this discrepancy. *i.* It has been suggested that Amestris and Esther are two ways of spelling the same name. 'The tendency to shorten foreign names, particularly when their etymology is not known, is widespread. The Greek name "Alexander" was widely adopted as "Sander".'[5] *ii.* Whatever the merits of the linguistic argument, on historical grounds the identification is impossible, as J. S. Wright points out: 'Since the third son of Xerxes and Amestris, Artaxerxes I, was born about 483,

---

[1]*HPE*, p. 171.     [2]*HPE*, pp. 230f.
[3]A..T. Olmstead (*HPE*, p. 168) includes a translation of the relevant section and full details of the publications bearing on the discoveries.
[4]*The Histories* vii. 61, 113.
[5]Robert Gordis, 'Religion, Wisdom and History in the Book of Esther – A New Solution to an Ancient Crux', *JBL* 100. 3 (September, 1981), p. 384.

Amestris cannot be identified with Esther who was not yet married.'[1] He goes on to argue that, given a Persian name which included 'V' and 'Sh', neither of which occurs in Greek, Vashti could have become Amestris. In view of the fact that the Persian name had already been Hebraized the identification is a possibility but cannot be more than that. But neither are we justified in assuming that the author of Esther was making up the story. The king was quite capable of taking a secondary wife; the official position of queen would not be jeopardized and her name would continue to appear in official records. That there is no extra-biblical evidence for Esther should not surprise us.

The derivation of the name Esther is disputed. The Hebrew *Hadassah* (2:7), meaning 'myrtle', evidently sounded like the Persian name which comes either from the Babylonian goddess, *Ishtar*, or from the Persian *sitâr*, 'star'. The Persian name would enable Esther to keep secret her foreign identity.

The name Mordecai is well authenticated as a personal name in the Persia of the fifth century BC, and appears in treasury tablets from Persepolis in a variety of forms. More particularly a man named Marduka is mentioned on an undated text, which probably belongs to the first two decades of the fifth century. He served as an accountant on an inspection tour from Susa, and therefore could be the biblical Mordecai, who regularly sat at the king's gate (2:19), like the Persian officials mentioned by Herodotus.[2] Even so it is impossible to know how likely it is that he should be identified with the character in the book of Esther, for there is no means of knowing how many other people bore the name. On the other hand Moore concludes that 'the epigraphic evidence concerning Marduka certainly prevents us from categorically ruling out as pure fiction the Mordecai episodes in the Book of Esther'.

### c. Purim

A number of issues connected with the origin of Purim have clouded the historical question for many writers. According to the book of Esther, which purports to explain how the annual festival originated, the casting of lots to find propitious

[1] *NPOT*, pp. 40f. Ctesias xiii. 51 is the source of information about the children.
[2] *The Histories* iii. 120. On the name Mordecai, C. A. Moore, 'Archaeology and the Book of Esther', *BA* 38 (1975), pp. 73f.

dates for important events was customary in Persia, and the word *pūr* is given its meaning, 'the lot' (3:7). In Hebrew the term was *gôrāl*, 'stone', for the practice of throwing a kind of dice in order to decide certain issues was known also in Israel (*cf.* Lv. 16:8; Nu. 26:55; Ps. 22:18), but the word *pūr* would not be generally known.

That explanation has not altogether convinced scholars, who have put forward their own theories for the origin of the festival, and at least in this particular have rejected the historicity of the book of Esther. The explanation in 9:26, 'Therefore they called these days Purim, after the term Pur', has struck many as strained. Evidence is drawn in support from the reference to the festival as the day of Mordecai in 2 Maccabees 15:36, and in Greek versions of Esther and in Josephus as *Phrourai*. Add to this evidence the pagan nature of the celebrations, when drinking was encouraged, and it is easy to see why some pagan source for the festival has been thought likely. 'Many scholars believe, therefore, that the word *pūrîm* represents a later folk etymology for a judaized pagan festival, that is, *pūrîm* (the Hebrew plural of *pūr*, "lot") was a name supplied by Babylonian Jews to a Jewish festival which had been initially pagan in both origin and character.'[1] Various ingenious alternative derivations have been suggested over the years from foreign words of doubtful assonance, none of which had anything to do with the casting of lots, and none of them has replaced the biblical explanation.[2]

In a recent lecture and article W. W. Hallo has drawn attention to a cube-shaped dice in the Yale collection, first published in 1937, and important for its inscription which twice uses the word *pūru*, 'lot'. It is known as 'the die of Iahali', a high official of Shalmaneser III, king of Assyria from 858 to 824 BC. 'It is the only cube that has survived to this day from the time when lots were cast annually in the selection and installation of the "eponym official", whose name was used in chronological tables to signify a certain year of a king's reign.'[3] As Hallo explains, 'We know that the fourth year of Shalmaneser's "second term" (like the 25th of his first) was

---

[1]So the prevailing opinion was summed up by C. A. Moore, *art. cit.*, p. 76.
[2]A summary occurs in W. W. Hallo, 'The First Purim', *BA* 46.1 (1983), p. 22.
[3]Part of a news release dated 21 April 1934, discovered by William Hallo and reprinted in *BA* 46.1 (1983), p. 27.

named after Iahali.'[1] Though the book of Esther belongs to Persia in the fifth century BC, and describes the use of the lot for a different purpose, nevertheless 'the terminology and the underlying technique remain the same'.[2] Thus the derivation of the word *pûrîm* given in the book is vindicated by the extraordinary chance of archaeology that one dice bearing the word *pûru* should come to light.

The dice serves a wider purpose, in that it illustrates how widespread was belief in a predetermined fate, with which it was considered important for men to co-operate if they were to succeed in their enterprises. Events for a year were predetermined on New Year's Day in Shalmaneser's reign, a fact which sheds light on Esther 3:7. Evidently on that day the court diary was still, some 350 years later, being filled in for the year with the help of dice, thrown to establish auspicious dates for all the known events. This detail removes one of the regularly cited problems of the book, and, by filling in background, forces a revision of previous misconceptions.

Given that the Jews lived in a fate-ridden culture while they inhabited Persia and the other lands of exile, we can readily appreciate that their theology needed to comprehend a belief in the power of their God to overrule the way the dice fell (Pr. 16:33). The book of Esther took the matter further: even when the dice had fallen the Lord was powerful to reverse its good omen into bad, in order to deliver his people.

An examination of the main historical allusions in Esther has affirmed the accuracy of many details. The events of the book can be harmonized with what is known from other sources about the reign of Ahasuerus, and, moreover, his character is recognizably the same. The extent of his empire, his capital, and the details of customs observed at court – such as the use of couriers on post-horses (3:13; 8:10), the prohibition of mourning (4:2) and hanging as the death penalty (5:14) – are examples of the genuinely Persian world in which the action takes place. The discovery of the word *pûru* on a dice has confirmed the dependence of the ancient world on the notion of destiny, and turned what once seemed 'historically improbable' as an account of the origin of Purim into an incident which has to be taken seriously.

By contrast, however, there are features of the story that

[1]*Ibid.*, p. 20.     [2]*Ibid.*, p. 22.

**CORBAN COLLEGE**

continue to seem improbable. The months of feasting (1:4), the year's beauty preparation (2:12), the height of Haman's scaffold (5:14) and the large numbers killed by the Jews (9:16) are obvious examples. In addition the plot depends on a network of strange coincidences which in the nature of the case are unverifiable, and which many scholars reckon to be characteristic of fiction rather than of historical events. On the other hand scholars continue to judge that the book has a historical nucleus. R. Gordis, for example, reckons that 'there is nothing intrinsically impossible or improbable in the central incident, when the accretions due to the storyteller's art are set aside'.[1] But the evidence is ambiguous, and judgments inconclusive. The importance of the book for modern historians can be gauged by the fact that, whereas Josephus included the Esther story in his *Antiquities of the Jews*, Martin Noth in his *History of Israel* makes no mention of it, and Geo Widengren dismisses it in thirteen lines. 'It is without much historical value.'[2] John Bright mentions the book by name but that is all.[3] Whatever others say, in practice historians ignore the book of Esther. Whatever the reason for this neglect of the book may be, we are justified in assuming that present-day historians do not take seriously the threat it records to the very existence of the Jewish race.

### III. LITERARY FEATURES

A study of the historical accuracy of the book of Esther has taken us a certain way towards an understanding of the book, but it has proved inconclusive. Its literary excellence has often been remarked upon, and an appreciation of the writer's artistry and of his methods of attaining effects may prove to be of some help in discerning his purpose in writing. To make a literary appreciation of a book is one way into the mind of the author, his unconscious assumptions as well as his presuppositions. The words he uses, the recurring themes and the structure of his book, taken together, provide pointers to his message.

Only a limited number of biblical writings have as their

[1]'Religion, Wisdom and History in the Book of Esther', *JBL* 100.3 (September 1981), p. 388.
[2]J. H. Hayes and J. M. Miller (Eds.), *Israelite and Judean History* (SCM, 1977), p. 493.
[3]*A History of Israel* (SCM, 1972), p. 434.

setting a country other than the land of Israel/Judah. The Joseph narrative is an obvious example, and recent studies have examined the extent to which the book of Esther is modelled on the experiences of Joseph in Egypt.[1] The books of Ruth and Jonah bring together people of another culture and religion with Israelites who are endeavouring to live in obedience to the living God, while the book of Daniel, set in the court of Babylon in the early days of the exile, and including an incident from the Persian period, has background in common with Esther. The extent and significance of other similarities need to be assessed.

It is not surprising that literature born of enforced residence in alien lands should be written on similar themes, nor that acculturalization should be seen in its most acute form in the lives of public figures serving at court. On this last criterion Ruth and Jonah among the above-mentioned writings have least in common with Esther. Nevertheless they illustrate different attitudes in Israel to foreigners and, like the book of Esther, show that meaningful human relationships are possible across national barriers. Not only so; the Lord even works to bring them about. In each of these books the hand of God is shown to be at work in human affairs generally, not just in those of Israel, as though such departmentalizing of divine sovereignty were possible. He controls all history with the discernible purpose of establishing justice and effecting salvation. Like the book of Esther, Ruth has in the title-role a woman who, by obedient but courageous submission, plays her part in working out that salvation. Jonah, too, saves Nineveh. Stylistically the book of Ruth matches its theme. Foreshadowing and anticipation, contrast and balance play a significant part in conveying the message that things are not what they seem. What appear to the participants to be coincidences are shown in the long run to be evidences of God's hand at work; he is well able to surprise and re-establish those he has brought low. In Jonah the 'reversal' takes place in the

[1] This comparison is not new. Jewish tradition has linked the two stories, and at the end of the nineteenth century L. A. Rosenthal and P. Riessler contributed articles on the subject in *ZAW* (1895, 1896, 1897). Recent studies in English include S. Talmon, '*Wisdom* in the Book of Esther', *VT* 13 (1963), pp. 419–455; W. Lee Humphreys, 'The Motif of the Wise Courtier in the Old Testament' (Th.D. Dissertation, Union Theological Seminary, New York, 1970); Sandra Beth Berg, *The Book of Esther* (SBL Dissertation Series, Scholars Press, Missoula, 1979), pp. 123–142. I am particularly indebted to Berg's study in this section.

prophet himself, and the change is reflected in the second half of the narrative in which Jonah does as he is told. There is a balance in the two parts of the story, and a similar balance has been pointed out in the structure of Esther.[1]

Daniel 1–6 and the Joseph narratives demonstrate that an Israelite was capable of rising to power in a foreign court. It was a dangerous place to be, and threats to life and liberty arose, but through them God's saving acts were seen. Allegiance to God and to right need not be jeopardized by living in an idolatrous culture, and, with that priority secured, loyalty could be given to the foreign king. Though suffering was not avoided, right was vindicated, the Israelite hero was promoted, and in some cases enemies were punished.

The Joseph story has the largest number of linguistic affinities with Esther. Where the subject-matter is similar there are striking similarities of wording (*cf.* Gn. 41:42–43 with Est. 6:11; Gn. 39:10 with Est. 3:4; Gn. 44:34 with Est. 8:6). These include both vocabulary and grammatical construction, but individually the examples are not impressive, because they are so ordinary. It is only as these are viewed cumulatively that the possibility of dependence suggests itself. If the older story is well known it may suggest to the author a paradigm for the later situation, and he may deliberately 'borrow' the phraseology because its associations recall the kind of message he wants to convey.[2] The later writer also chose to use some of the same devices as the story-teller of the Joseph narrative, such as anticipation of events and interruption of the plot, so creating dramatic tension. God's activity is occasionally referred to in connection with Joseph's experiences (*cf.* Gn. 45:4–8), but omitted entirely in Esther. Berg concludes, 'with the exception of linguistic correspondences, most of the similarities between Joseph and Esther are of a general nature', and any precise account of the dependence of the book of Esther on the Joseph story is elusive. One suggestion is that the later writer wished to indicate that human initiative was essential for the successful outcome of events, and this

---

[1]Yehuda T. Radday, 'Chiasm in Joshua, Judges and Others', *LB* 3 (1973), p. 9. Quoted by Berg, p. 108.

[2]There is no need to go along with the view that the Joseph narrative was a post-exilic document, a *Diasporanovelle*, put forward, *e.g.*, by Arndt Meinhold in a doctoral dissertation (1969) and referred to by Berg, p. 142. See also 'Die Gattung der Josephgeschichte und des Estherbuches: Diasporanovelle, I, II.', *ZAW* 87 (1975), pp. 305–324; 88 (1976), pp. 79–93.

could well have been read from the Esther story.

The fact that these common themes occur in several biblical stories does not have to lead to the conclusion that they are imaginative tales without any factual basis. Present-day victims of oppression show a very natural preoccupation in their writings with the injustices they and others have suffered at the hands of their oppressors, but every kind of stylistic device may be used to bring home the message to the reader. The same is true of the biblical writers, whose message concerned Israelites beyond the borders of their own land. The miraculous did not occur in Esther; the time seemed long and uneventful, yet deliverance was granted. The events celebrated in the book were a kind of reassurance that, despite exile, there was still cause for hope. There could be an answer to the prayer of the Psalmist:

> We do not see our signs;
>     there is no longer any prophet,
>     and there is none among us who knows how long.
> How long, O God, is the foe to scoff? (Ps. 74:9–10)

### a. Themes

The book opens by introducing Ahasuerus; it does so in such a way as to lay stress on his extensive empire, his capital city of Susa and his personal wealth and power. King Ahasuerus was a man to be reckoned with. Though his style and the ideal of kingship in Israel (*cf.* Dt. 17:14–20) could hardly have been more different, Ahasuerus was powerful, whereas Israel's kings and kingdom were no more. The implied contrast has weight, and yet there is irony in chapter one. Despite the display of riches, glory, spendour and pomp (1:4) the queen defied his majesty, and every husband's authority was threatened. The author had other ideas of leadership, and a different yardstick by which to judge worth.

Closely associated with kingship is the theme of feasting. Ostensibly impressed with the magnificence of the newly built palace, the unlimited supplies and the months of entertainment, the author makes an implied contrast between the 180 days for the aristocratic visitors and the seven days for the local residents. And nothing good comes out of this feasting which brings about the downfall of the queen, and raises the question of a successor. Esther, too, holds two feasts, at the second of which Haman falls from power and meets his end.

Finally Mordecai institutes two days of feasting to be observed by all Jews. The despised and powerless exiles have shared in the exaltation to power of Esther and Mordecai, through whom they have been saved from death. Now people were in awe of them (8:17; 9:2). These three parallel occasions for feasting, spread as they are from the beginning to the middle and end of the story, argue for its unity and illustrate role reversal.

A further theme, scarcely less obvious, is that of conflicting loyalties. As residents of the Persian empire the Jews owed allegiance to the king, but they also committed themselves to uphold the traditions of the community of their fellow countrymen, scattered in every province. Conflict began when the king's favourite expected all to prostrate themselves before him. Mordecai's refusal is stated but not explained, except in so far as Mordecai's Jewishness was an explanation (3:4). To Haman it was a personal insult, whereas to Mordecai it was a matter of conscience, a familiar enough conflict in most walks of life. Yet Mordecai had already proved his loyalty to the king (2:19–23). The insubordination of Mordecai brought about the mortal threat which required Esther to disobey the king (4:11). Her natural desire to conform and obey was confronted by the need to save her people from death. The author presented the conflicting claims and indicated that obedience to king and husband had to give way before the overriding importance of life for God's people (though he did not call them that). Once convinced that she must identify herself with the need of her people, Esther acted with courage and became in her own right (and not just as the ward of Mordecai) a leader who took initiatives and saved the situation. Civil disobedience of a minor nature is seen to be justified in a greater cause, namely, the genuine good of the state (7:4). The author is convinced that loyalty both to temporal ruler and to eternal principles is possible in an alien state, though it may involve conflict.

Between the banquets of the king and those of Esther the contrary theme of fasting is twice introduced (4:1–3, 16). Fasting as well as feasting took place in company with others, and demonstrated the solidarity of all Jews in facing the threat to their nation. Their mourning garments, noisy laments and public gatherings ensured that their protests were observed by the rest of the population, who registered disquiet (3:15), and later their support (8:15, 17). Ordinary citizens were sympathetic, in the eyes of the writer correctly assessing where justice lay. When Esther had to risk her life by invading the king's throne room on behalf of her people, she wished to do so with their total support. The three-day fast in which all participated demonstrated that they stood or fell together. Esther's banquet (2:18) is followed by Esther's fast (4:16).

The contrast between fasting and feasting, and perhaps the importance of what happens during the fasting as a key to the events of the feasting, are maintained in the institution of Purim. Though rejoicing is the main emphasis, fasting is also to be recapitulated in the commemorative annual event (9:31). Though the feasts are more prominent than the fasts, as they would have been in court life, it is in connection with the fasts that the turning-point comes in the story (4:14). The words of Mordecai imply that life is no mere random collection of incidents, but, in the hands of an unseen guide, a purposeful journey, during which the individual fulfils an intended role. A hopeful outcome to the fast is therefore anticipated, and could be implied in the commemorative fasts of future crises.

Several other themes could profitably be followed through, such as the role of law (Heb. *dāt*, which occurs elsewhere in the Old Testament only in Dt. 33:2; Ezr. 8:36); the bestowal of gifts by the king, omission of which in 2:23 is made good in 6:6, to Haman's dismay; and the part played in the book by 'coincidences'. I believe it would be true to say that a study of literary themes has done more to promote an understanding of the book than all the discussions about historicity, which so occupied scholars earlier this century. 'If Scripture is approached only as history, interpreters of Scripture are doomed to live in the past or, what amounts to the same thing, to try to reproduce the past in the present. This is impossible to do.'[1] The predominant themes of a book and the way the author handles them take the reader close to the eternal dimension of Scripture.

### b. Structure

Mention of themes that recur in the book has already had a bearing on its structure, suggesting that it conforms to a pattern. Part of the task of the reader is to discern whether there is such a pattern, and, if so, what it indicates about the

[1] James G. Williams, *Women Recounted: Narrative Thinking and the God of Israel*, p. 13. Though Williams may exaggerate a little he still makes a valuable point.

author's message. The book of Esther, having first set the scene, begins to indicate that all is not well in Susa. Various strands are interwoven to produce this impression, the dominant one being the hatred of Haman that threatens to exterminate the Jews. The death of Haman instead of Mordecai, and the killing of the enemies of the Jews, are the unexpected outcome of a sequence of 'coincidences'. In order to determine the structure it is necessary to decide the turning-point in the plot. It is tempting to look for a half-way mark, such as the king's sleepless night (6:1–3), which comes between Esther's two feasts and would provide a centre round which the symmetry of the structure could be built. This has already been demonstrated to produce a credible result, as the diagram shows.

Opening and background (chapter 1)
The king's first decree (2,3)                        } Mortal
The clash between Haman and Mordecai (4,5)      Danger

'On that night the king could not sleep' (6:1) → Crisis

Mordecai's triumph over Haman (6,7)
The king's second decree (8,9)                      } Salvation
Epilogue (10)[1]

There is, of course, the possibility of overlooking important factors in a search for a 'pattern', which has been arrived at only by a process of over-simplification. There is need therefore to investigate further to see whether more detailed analysis supports the proposed general structure. This also has been done, to the extent of showing that in the Hebrew the wording of pairs of sentences links together earlier and later events (*e.g.* 3:1 with 10:3; 3:7 with 9:24).[2] These two examples show that the author is careful to tie up the ends, but not necessarily more than that. Other examples are built more securely into the fabric, and show the 'reversal' theme worked out (*e.g.* 3:10 with 8:2a; 3:12–13 with 8:9–11; 3:14 with 8:13). There is nothing artificial about these comparisons; the events happen twice and similar wording comes twice, but the author could have varied his way of expressing himself. The fact that he chose to repeat his phraseology supports the view that he was deliberately drawing attention to the contrast

[1] Yehuda T. Radday, 'Chiasm in Joshua, Judges and Others', *LB* 3 (1973), p. 9. Reproduced by Berg, p. 108.
[2] Berg, pp. 106f. She uses the work of M. Fox.

between what had been expected and the eventual outcome. One weakness is the concentration of examples in chapters 3 and 8. Though not confined to these chapters the examples would better support the structure if they occurred more widely.

A comparison of words and phrases lends some support to the argument that the author was structuring his work as an example of expectations reversed. Balancing episodes also tend to support this thesis: three banquets take place in the first half of the book and three in the second; the royal chronicles are referred to at the beginning (2:23), middle (6:1) and end (10:2).[1] But, as Radday himself admits, the stylistic elements do not occur in the inverse order which chiastic structure strictly demands.[2] If, however, the writer is recording events that were well known to some at least of his readers, there were limits to his freedom in rearranging them. In any case it was the events themselves that dictated the structure; what happened in the end was the opposite of what was originally expected, and that raises the question why that should have been so. Is the writer drawing attention to the unseen hand of Providence at work, as for example in causing sleep to retreat from the king (6:1), so explaining why that verse is the central point? Or is he showing the part played by human decisions in the outworking of history, in which case the turning-point would be located in chapter 4, when Esther agrees to risk her life (16)? The emphasis on communal fasting, however, negates the suggestion that everything depends on one woman. Moreover fasting implied dependent prayer, imploring divine aid. As Berg points out it is from this point on that 'the series of "theses" ends and the sequence of "antitheses" begins. Here, Mordecai obeys Esther, reversing our images of the protagonists. Esther becomes the initiator of events, and this transition is marked by Ahasuerus' rewarding, not punishing, her crime in 5:1–5.'[3] The inference is not so much that human intervention shapes events as that human admission of weakness and need brings about a reversal which, in the light of the world's power struggles, has far-reaching implications for history. The expected course of events could suddenly be reversed in favour of the oppressed. In prospect

---

[1] Y. T. Radday, *art. cit.*, p. 9.
[2] The structure of Zechariah shows this. *Cf.* J. G. Baldwin, *Haggai, Zechariah, Malachi* (TOTC, 1972), pp. 85f.; see also 'Structure', pp. 74–81.
[3] Berg, p. 110.

nothing seemed less likely, hence Esther's preparedness for the worst to happen, 'If I perish, I perish' (4:16). Nor could any ground for hope be argued (*cf.* Dn. 3:17–18). Nevertheless the author evidently believed that he was doing more than relate one isolated and unrepeatable example of deliverance.

Every good story presents a problem, however, and indicates how it is solved. Esther is no exception. Looked at from one point of view the solution is unexpected; from another the events and scenes follow a natural sequence. In other words the author has chosen his scenes so skilfully that the action is close-knit and convincing. The resulting structure permits the reader to see how the writer perceived events, the selection, both of incidents and of phraseology, indicating the balance between expectation and outcome, and leaving the reader to make his own deductions as to what this contrast says about history in general. Subsequent generations have not done him justice.

## IV. LITERARY GENRE

Into what category of literature does this book of Esther best fit? The question may seem to be academic, and yet it is another approach to the world of the author, his presuppositions and purpose in writing, and an approach which has been popular with recent scholars. More important, our understanding of the book depends to a large extent upon appreciating the type of literature it is.

Earliest Jewish exegesis of the period *c.* 200 BC to AD 200 developed along two lines; there was *halaka*, which indicated how one should 'walk', and *haggada*, which filled out the narrative sections of Scripture. The book of Esther was considered to fall into both categories; it was both law and history, and was the authoritative source from which the proper observance of Purim could be deduced. But since Christians did not observe Purim the book had little to say to them, and 'not a single Christian commentary was written on this book during the first seven centuries of our era'.[1] Indeed, it was not until the Reformation period that serious commentaries of lasting worth were produced, and these assumed the book to be strictly historical. Luther and Calvin left no commentaries on Esther.

[1] L. B. Paton, *ICC*, p. 101.

When the Enlightenment burst upon Europe in the middle of the eighteenth century and brought its rationalistic influence to bear on biblical exegesis, previously held views were called in question. Ever since then doubts have been expressed as to the historical worth of Esther, and this question has remained the centre of debate between more traditional and more radical scholars almost to the present time. Most have taken the view that there is only a vestige of history in the book, though a few have argued for complete historicity.[1] S. R. Driver accepted that there were improbabilities in the story, 'though the narrative cannot reasonably be doubted to have a substantial historical basis'.[2]

At the other end of the spectrum there are a few writers who judge the book to be a fabrication, a point of view represented by R. H. Pfeiffer, who would put Ruth, Jonah and Daniel in the same category. Writing in the 1940s he confidently asserted that the majority of critics had come to the conclusion that the story of Esther is not history but fiction.[3] He admits that the character of Xerxes resembles that depicted in other sources, and that the incidents related do not contradict the history of his reign, but notes numerous 'highly improbable' details which he considers to be characteristic of fiction, and the result of thorough research on the part of the novelist. Though Pfeiffer considers it idle to speculate on the possibility that some incidents may be based on fact because such guesses lack all confirmation, he naively assumes the correctness of his own guess that the 'coincidences, the artificiality of the plot and the transparent purpose' establish the work as fiction.

However the scene may have appeared in the 1940s, more recent writers have not altogether followed the radical stance of Pfeiffer in relation to this book, though the influence of his view continues to be apparent. L. H. Brockington, for example, is impressed with the fictional quality of many of the details, including the names of the characters.[4] But he

[1]Among those who have judged the book to be historical are C. F. Keil (1870); A. H. Sayce (1885), though he changed his opinion in 1893; J. Hoshander (1923); J. B. Schildenberg (1941); J. S. Wright (1970); R. Gordis (1981).
[2]*LOT*, p. 483.
[3]*PIOT*, pp. 737–740. He writes, 'The accuracy of some of the local colour proves only that the author knew nearly as much about Persian culture as modern archaeologists' (p. 740). He could, after all, have lived in Susa!
[4]*CeB*, pp. 217–220.

acknowledges the author's wide knowledge of local customs, and classifies his book as a historical novel, thus making the best of both points of view, the historical and the fictional. Not that the classification was new, for it had been suggested long before.[1] It is still the judgment most frequently supported by commentators.

In view of the popularity of historical novels in Europe during the nineteenth century, the suggestion is a natural one, if more than a little anachronistic. Support for it was found in the stories of Judith and Tobit in the Apocrypha, as well as in the semi-historical tales of Persian literature. Nevertheless it was a far cry from these examples of ancient stories to the modern historical novel, and there were vast differences between the ancient tales, such that the Hebrew Esther was accepted as being in a class apart from the other two.[2] As B. W. Anderson remarks in connection with the inclusion of Esther but not Judith in the canon of Scripture, 'there is a certain wisdom and significance in the fact that Esther appears in the canon of Scripture, which the church claims to be the word of God'.[3] He sees the book, irrespective of its genre, as itself 'a valuable historical witness to the Jewish struggle for survival in the post-exilic period'.[4]

One of the most obvious differences between historical novels and these ancient books is their length, and there is much to be said for thinking in terms of the short story (German *Novelle*), and, since Esther is set in Persia among the scattered exiles, *Diasporanovelle* is a likely category to come to mind.[5] In addition, since the story is concerned with the

---

[1]See, for example, A. H. Sayce, *The Higher Criticism, and the Verdict of the Monuments* (1893), pp. 469 ff.; W. F. Adeney, *EB*, p. 354; A. W. Streane, *CB*, pp. xiv f.

[2]*Cf.* 'Text and Versions of Esther', pp. 42–48, below.

[3]'The Place of the Book of Esther in the Christian Bible', *Journal of Religion* 30 (1950), p. 34.

[4]*Ibid.*, p. 39, footnote.

[5]*Cf.* p. 26, n.2. There are aspects of the *Novelle* (a type of literature which has not been developed in English) which could make it appropriate for Esther. It restricts itself to a single event, which it tends to present as 'chance', and the function of the *Novelle* is to reveal that, in reality, the event is due to 'fate'. The outworking of the event reveals qualities of character in the persons concerned which were latent in them, and its action must take place in the world of reality. Its starting-point could be an actual event. It deals with a striking subject and in its structure has a turning-point which moves the narrative in an unexpected direction. *Cf.* E. K. Bennett, *The History of the German Novelle* (Cambridge, ²1961).

origin of Purim, it has been called a 'festival legend'.[1] These descriptive titles are less helpful than attempts to find a general category, such as that of Talmon to link Esther with Wisdom literature.[2] His suggestion that it is a historicized wisdom tale, illustrating the outcome of applied maxims accepted by the wise, whatever their race, would set the book in the wider context of internationally recognized, pragmatic understanding of the world and its laws. It would also help to explain the strange absence of the name of God and all reference to prayer and other religious practices. In this respect it contributes to a possible way of understanding the book and of accounting for one of its most puzzling aspects, namely the omission of any reference to the land of Israel or any of its sacred institutions. Talmon insists that 'the presentation in traditional wisdom imagery does not necessarily impair the possible authenticity of the historical situation which is described in the book'.[3] In other words historical incidents lend themselves to presentation in wisdom 'dress', so that Talmon's 'historicized wisdom tale' leaves open the question whether the events narrated actually happened. The strongest argument against Talmon's thesis rests on the clear insistence in other wisdom books of the Bible that the Lord is the source of wisdom (*e.g.* Pr. 1:7; Jb. 28:28), and God directs all aspects of human life (Ec. 2:24–26). The same is true of the Joseph narrative, which is referred to frequently in wisdom terms. Why then should the author of Esther studiously avoid references to the Lord God of Israel?

The further suggestion has recently been put forward that, coming as it most probably does from a Persian setting, the book is written in the style of a Persian chronicle composed by a Gentile scribe.[4] As such it is in a class apart among the books of the Bible, argues Gordis. The Jewish author, assuming the role of a pagan chronicler, avoids all reference to the beliefs and practices of his people, yet indirectly testifies to his faith (Est. 4:14). Appropriately Mordecai is called 'the Jew'; his people are referred to throughout in the third person (*e.g.* 9:15); Ahasuerus is given due honour and his counsellors

---

[1]H. Ringgren, *ATD* 16 (1967), pp. 371–404, especially 375.
[2]S. Talmon, 'Wisdom in the Book of Esther', *VT* 13 (1963), pp. 419–455.
[3]*Ibid.*, p. 453.
[4]Robert Gordis, 'Religion, Wisdom and History in the Book of Esther – A New Solution to an Ancient Crux', *JBL* 100.3 (1981), pp. 359–388, especially pp. 375–378.

are named (1:10, 14); the listing of the sons of Haman would be in keeping with an official chronicle (9:7–10); and the heaping up of formulae (*cf.* 1:22; 3:12; 4:3) reflects the age-old style of legal documents. By writing as if he were a Persian scribe the writer seeks to buttress confidence in the veracity of his narrative and thus help to establish Purim as a universally observed Jewish holiday, though it did not originate in Palestine.

There is much to be said in favour of this suggestion of Gordis. Admittedly 'no historical chronicles, royal or otherwise, for the Achaemenid period (550–331 B.C.E.) have survived', so there is no means of checking how well our author succeeded in reproducing their style.[1] We know, however, that other biblical writers, especially the historians, drew on official chronicles, and the rapid unfolding of events without reference to motives is what one would expect in an official chronicle. Gordis thinks that in 3:13 there is a citation of the salient words of Haman's edict, repeated again when it is countermanded by Mordecai (8:11).[2] The effect of putting into quotation marks the citation from Haman's edict is to mitigate one of the ethical objections to the book, for, though the Jews were empowered to fight their foes (9:2), they killed only men (Heb. *'îš*) and took no booty (9:12, 15). 'The book is hostile only to Haman and his supporters, and not to the king, his court, or the general population.'[3]

Though it is still not possible to establish for certain the genre of the book of Esther, recent studies have opened up new ways of understanding it, which incline towards a greater appreciation of its contribution to Scripture.

### V. THEOLOGY

It is likely to seem at first sight an anomaly to seek for the theology of a book which does not even mention the name of God. The fact has long caused offence. The only other Old Testament book of which this is true is the Song of Songs, but there in the Hebrew the name Yah has been discerned (8:6).[4]

[1] *Ibid.*, p. 375, footnote.
[2] *Ibid.*, p. 377. *Cf.* R. Gordis, 'Studies in the Esther Narrative', *JBL* 95 (1976), p. 52.
[3] *JBL* 95 (1976), p. 52.
[4] The suffix of the word *šalhebetyâ*, 'most vehement flame', lit. 'Yahweh flame' (BDB, p. 529a). *Cf.* G. Lloyd Carr, *The Song of Solomon* (*TOTC*, 1984), pp. 170f.

There is a veiled reference to the deity in Esther 4:14, 'relief and deliverance will rise for the Jews from another quarter' (Heb. *māqôm*), but even when prayer to him is the natural purpose of fasting, still that is not made explicit. Reactions to this deficiency in the book have been along two lines. *i*. The Greek translators added extensive passages, three of which seem to have been designed to make more explicit the work of God, who gives guidance by dreams and answers prayer. *ii*. Others have considered the book to have no place in the canon of Scripture; a few, including Luther, have said so explicitly, but many more have virtually omitted it from consideration. If the book of Esther has a place in the Christian Scriptures it is important to appreciate the contribution it makes to the total Old Testament revelation, and to the Bible as a whole.

It is easy to see why the book is valued by Jews, who have suffered so much through the ages and have clung to the assurance implied by Purim that, however severe the threat upon their race, they have a future. 'God was not overt, His word not direct, and His face not revealed, still, behind the veil of *purim*, God's providence towards His people, would uphold them against adversary and ideological force alike, as in Passover of old.'[1] No wonder the story has delighted and uplifted Jewish hearts, giving them hope even in the darkest days. It has played its part in maintaining what Kenneth Cragg refers to as 'this transcendent quality of Israel's assurance of right, . . . which makes Palestinian struggle in any contrary sense so *a priori* unequal, short of a similar mystique of destiny.' 'Zionism proper . . . has those very imponderables which . . . Israel harnesses and urges so tenaciously – sacred history, divine charter, mysterious destiny – and the Holocaust.'[2] To this day, therefore, the annual reading of the book of Esther at Purim generates unfailing enthusiasm and keeps alive Jewish belief in God's continuing providence, despite all the victimization. In Jewish eyes the book lives.

There are two conflicting world-views in the book, one represented by Haman, who believes in chance-fate and thinks that on this basis he can annihilate God's people. In other words he is a practical atheist, and the writer portrays his

[1]Abraham D. Cohen, "'Hu Ha-goral": The Religious Significance of Esther', *Judaism* 23 (1974), p. 94.
[2]Kenneth Cragg, *This Year in Jerusalem* (Darton, Longman and Todd, 1982), p. 136.

world only to parody it. Put in a position of power he uses it to further his own ends, while at the same time giving the impression that he is concerned for the king's interests (3:8). Not that he stands to gain by his ruse; money is no object and he is already second only to the king. Rather, his pique will find expression, and the outrage on his dignity will be avenged. The suffering intended is out of all proportion to the cause, but petty-minded self-importance can brook no opposition and makes no attempt to account for it. Haman takes for granted his own ability to engineer events and bring about his hostile intentions. He believes he can control history within the limits of his cirumstances.

The other world-view also lays stress on human initiative. Mordecai urged Esther to approach the king; if she failed to make this move, dangerous as it was, her own life and the life of her people could be wiped out. Thus human responsibility continues to be prominent, but it is not isolated from the conviction that events are part of a pattern for which only the Lord God could be responsible. True, he is not named, but when Mordecai says to Esther, 'And who knows whether you have to come to the kingdom for such a time as this?' (4:14) he is revealing his belief in an overruling of history. Esther's choice as queen had been no random chance, but the work of the Director of world affairs, so that through her this act of deliverance could be effected.

The book sets the two world-views in contrast, and shows by the outcome which is to be preferred. Whereas Haman was hung on his own gallows, Mordecai took Haman's place of power (8:2). As for the Jews, despite the laws intended for their downfall, they were permitted to live and put to death their foes. The tables were turned; retributive justice was seen to be done. But it was the king who, in response to the information given by Harbona, said 'Hang him [Haman] on that' (7:10), and who promoted Mordecai to power. Human agents were the unwitting instruments of one who was the unseen Ruler of events.

According to this second world-view the Jews had a special place in the divine purpose, and even Haman's wife, Zeresh, had heard tell that those who tried to prevail over the Jews would fall before them (6:13). Mordecai's conviction was that, even if Esther failed to buy up her opportunity of influence, 'relief and deliverance for the Jews' would arise from somewhere else (4:14), so certain was he that their destruction would not be permitted. Despite centuries of anti-Semitism, culminating in the Nazi Holocaust, deliberate attempts to destroy the Jews have failed. Belief in God's purpose for them had evidently not been misplaced, whether they were in Jerusalem or scattered to the ends of the earth.

Observance of Purim has played its part in keeping alive Jewish hopes. It has also fed nationalistic aims which in turn have tended to encourage Jewish suspicions of 'Christians'. Residents from Susa are likely to have been among the Parthians and Medes and Elamites who witnessed the first outpouring of God's Spirit (Acts 2:9). Those Jews who believed ceased to observe Purim, and became part of the wider community of the church. What then does the book of Esther say to Christians?

In the past the book has not seemed important to Christians, as we have already shown.[1] Its Judaizing tendency was obvious, whereas its Christian content was not. We may begin, however, by asking whether the purpose of God in so marvellously protecting the Jews sheds light on its significance. Within the book itself the last verse gives something of a clue, in that Mordecai 'sought the welfare of his people and spoke peace to all his people'; his leadership was marked by prosperity, and resulted in contentment throughout the realm. Good though that was, it is unlikely to have been the total reason for Jewish deliverance. Nehemiah, cupbearer in Susa to the successor of Ahasuerus, appealed to Deuteronomy, with its strong theological interpretation of the Exodus deliverance (Ne. 1:5–9; *cf.* Dt. 30:1–4). His ground of appeal was the character of their 'great and terrible God who keeps covenant' (Ne. 1:5), and if the writer of Esther was a Jew, as he almost certainly was, this would have been his faith also, though he does not disclose it. If we press the question of the purpose of the covenant, as expounded at its simplest it was that Abraham's nation should become great and be a blessing to all the families of the earth (Gn. 12:3). No doubt Israel was a blessing in many ways, standing as it did for righteousness, exemplified at Israel's best in impressive lives, but overall the story was disappointing until the Christ came and transformed the promise into fulfilment. Yet, by confrontation with Gentiles, Jewish particularity has become more entrenched; having failed to find in Jesus the Messiah, Jews have become

[1]See above, p. 32.

'stranded', knowing their identity and yet finding little positive satisfaction in it.

The book of Esther belongs at the end of Old Testament revelation, and shows how Jews, far away geographically from Jerusalem and its Temple, nevertheless saw themselves as essentially one with their Israelite kith and kin, for whom they were prepared to die. Esther and Mordecai were providentially placed at the heart of the Persian empire with power to act politically on behalf of their people. It would appear from the reluctance with which the book was accepted in Jerusalem as part of the canon that their brothers who spent their days in study of the law and in Temple liturgy were unimpressed.[1] A rift was appearing between the orthodox religious Jews who had given their lives to rebuilding Zion and those who remained among the Gentiles, feathering their own nests. It has never entirely healed. Yet the book of Esther shows that God has his purpose in exalting some among his own to places of power and influence. He is at work there as well as in the worship, prayer and study of Scripture. Christians also have a way of painting in glowing colours those who are in certain kinds of 'full-time' work, whereas God's calling is to all, whether in sacred or secular spheres, and no one group has a monopoly of his service or of his blessing.

The remarkable part played by providential 'coincidences' in the Esther story is both heartening and humbling, yet it also needs to be accompanied by a certain caution. It is heartening because the God of the Bible could well be named the God of coincidences. If those scientists are right who incorporate in their account of creation the law of natural selection, that law must have operated on million-to-one chances to produce the world we know, while in our personal lives there are occasions when interlinked coincidences are too extraordinary to be put down to mere chance. The right reaction, however, is not to assume that for some reason God is on our side and will continue to give us on a plate all the good things we request, but rather to be in awe that the mighty God should condescend to answer our prayers despite our many shortcomings and downright failures. The sense of wonder should result in more whole-hearted commitment to his service. The caution is necessary when, as a result of observing God's good hand at work in the past, one presumes

---

[1] See 'The canonical status of Esther', pp. 49–52, below.

to know his mind in all other situations.

An example occurred in the famous stand against the Romans made by the Jews at Masada in AD 73. Believing themselves to be inviolate, the defenders took up their position in the mountain stronghold overlooking the Dead Sea, but the Romans doggedly pursued their aim to defeat them, and the 960 Jews took their own life rather than surrender. 'It had been proper indeed for us to have conjectured at the purpose of God much sooner . . .' said Eleazar, as he proposed suicide to the defenders.[1] The incident stands alongside defeats recorded in the Old Testament: the defeat at Ai (Jos. 7:2–5), and the fall of both Samaria and Jerusalem in particular, when it seemed that God had gone back on his word. As it turned out in all three cases, the fault lay in Israel's disobedience. In the Maccabean struggle as in Esther, Gentile arrogance against the Jews was tantamount to an attack on their God, who defended his people by giving them victory. What was wrong at Masada? What was wrong at Jerusalem in AD 70? Only now has the Jew regained a land and a state after all the centuries, a right which he sees to have been granted as a counterpart to the Holocaust, and in the granting of which, 'at several critical junctures in the story Arab attitudes greatly facilitated Jewish purposes and so aided and abetted the aims of Israel'. That it should have been so confirmed in some Israeli eyes the assurance of divine 'intendedness' about Israel.[2] Was the 'coincident' aspect of Esther being repeated?

The difficulty is that 'divine right' puts a matter beyond argument and sets every other right out of consideration. Perhaps this is why the author of Esther kept his story on the human plane, aware of divine destiny, but not making grand claims. Events themselves required an explanation and he deemed it best to let them speak for themselves, leaving the reader to make his own deductions.

The book of Esther, like other books of the post-exilic period, was probing for answers to new questions. What future was there for Jews in scattered groups within an alien empire? Was their God with them, and if so what did he require of them? The writer of Esther could affirm that God was indeed with them, and it followed that they should continue to be true to him and loyal to their gentile kings. Purim celebrated

[1] Flavius Josephus, *Wars of the Jews* vii. 6.
[2] Kenneth Cragg, *This Year in Jerusalem*, p. 133.

41

their deliverance from death, which, like the Passover, should have alerted them to look for an even greater salvation. Some may have found it when they made a pilgrimage to Jerusalem in about AD 30, and heard a certain Peter preaching in the open air to a huge multi-national crowd.

The book of Esther encourages us to expect that, like the Jewish people in the fifth century BC, our contemporaries can discover, if they will, evidence of God's working in their personal circumstances as well as in recent history. Two events stand out in the war of 1939–1945: the extraordinary deliverance of Britain at Dunkirk, and the final allied victory. The survival of the state of Israel requires an explanation. Here is a fact of history which seems to witness to a divine overruling of events even more extraordinary than those 'coincidences' of the Esther story. Controversial and painful as the interpretation may be, the fact itself cannot be ignored. The unseen hand behind the events in Susa is no less active in guiding history today. The book of Esther is still relevant.

## VI. TEXT AND VERSIONS OF ESTHER

No other book of the Old Testament has come down to us in so many variant forms. It is not only that translations were current in major languages of the Jewish Diaspora, but that there were evidently different originals behind alternative versions within language groups, and in some cases omissions and additions of considerable length have to be accounted for. Nor is this merely an academic conundrum, of interest only to the scholar, though the intricacies of source material can be obscure. It has a bearing on our reading of the New Testament, because we discover that the Scriptures of those who wrote its books were not absolutely identical with our Old Testament, and an account of the vicissitudes of the book of Esther can serve as a reminder that a complicated history lies behind the canon of Scripture.

1. *Hebrew and closely related texts.* Many manuscripts of Esther are available in Hebrew, the language in which the book was originally written, partly because every Jewish family has traditionally wished to own a copy from which to read at Purim, but no extant Hebrew MS is earlier than the eleventh century AD. Thanks to the painstaking way in which textual traditions were preserved by the Massoretes and their successors, there are no significant differences between these copies;

even the Babylonian text presents no variations in the consonantal text of Esther. 'In the vocalization and accentuation it contains unimportant differences that do not affect the sense of a single passage.'[1] That there is no evidence for the Hebrew text earlier than the eleventh century AD is accounted for by the fact that no single trace of the book of Esther has been found at Qumran, and the great uncial MSS, such as Codex Sinaiticus, were in Greek.

Closely related to the Hebrew is the Syriac version, assessed by Paton as 'an extremely faithful translation of the original. Here and there a word is added for the sake of clearness, but ordinarily H [the Hebrew] is followed with slavish fidelity. When possible, the translator even uses the same root that appears in Heb.'[2] There are, however, some variants on the MT, though the translation must have been made from a text very similar to it.

Aramaic translations of the Hebrew Scriptures became necessary as early as the fourth century BC (and even earlier; *cf.* Ne. 8:7–8, 'the Levites . . . gave the sense'), and these were based on oral explanations given in the synagogues. The First Targum, or translation into biblical Aramaic, of Esther incorporates comments that are very ancient, and which may, indeed, have been handed down from the last centuries before the Christian era. The text is a faithful translation of the Hebrew, to which all sorts of extra material have been added, from grammatical points to fanciful interpretations, so doubling the length of the narrative. The Second Targum translates the Hebrew literally, which aids reconstruction of the Hebrew used by the translator, and adds so many embellishments to the text that it becomes four times its original length. Since this Second Targum shows evidence of borrowings from the First it must be later; indeed it appears to conflate several explanations, which in some cases contradict one another. 'Only where T² runs parallel to the Heb. has it any value for the text, the additions are all late *midrash* that never existed in any other language than Aramaic.'[3]

2. *Greek.* The conquests of Alexander the Great brought the biblical lands into the sphere of Greek culture and language by the end of the fourth century BC. Within a generation or two the need was evident for a translation of the Hebrew Scriptures into Greek, and by the middle of the third century

[1]*ICC*, p. 16.     [2]*ICC*, p. 17.     [3]*ICC*, p. 24.

BC the translation of the Pentateuch was probably completed. According to popular tradition based on a 'Letter of Aristeas' the translation of the Law was commissioned by Ptolemy II Philadelphus (285–247 BC) in Alexandria. Seventy translators were commissioned for the work, hence the name 'Septuagint', from the Latin for seventy, and the abbreviation LXX. The translation of other books followed, and by 132 BC, when the grandson of Jesus ben Sira was writing his Foreword to the Greek translation of Ecclesiasticus (*cf.* the reference to 'my grandfather' in the prologue), he could refer to 'the Law and the Prophets and the others that followed them', that is, the three-part division of the Hebrew canon was by his time translated into Greek.

It is clear that, if the Hebrew presupposed by the LXX could be reconstructed, it would provide a witness to a pre-Christian form of that text. This reconstruction, however, is no simple process and, though it has occupied the detailed attention of many scholars over the years, the task is by no means completed. Already in the third century AD there were many Greek translations of the Old Testament, and Origen was prompted by this multiplicity to construct a critical edition, by means of which to compare different versions with the Hebrew original. This he did by employing six columns, hence the name *Hexapla*, in which he set side by side the Hebrew text, his own Greek transliteration, and four Greek texts in use by the church. In the book of Esther his column five, which contained the LXX, would have had to include whole paragraphs which were not in the Hebrew, and occasionally LXX omitted material present in the Hebrew. The versions used by Origen and other early translations are known mainly from quotations, though Origen's fifth column was translated literally into Syriac, and since the major part of this survives it bears witness to his LXX text. Of the *Hexapla* only fragments remain.

In modern times LXX critical study owes much to the work of Paul de Lagarde, whose attempts to establish the original Greek version of Genesis to Esther were published in 1883. 'Only for the book of Esther . . . did LAGARDE print the texts of "the Lucianic", or A-text, and the traditional Septuagint, or B-text, side by side for purposes of comparison.'[1] His work is

---

[1] Carey A. Moore, 'A Greek Witness to a Different Hebrew Text of Esther', *ZAW* 79 (1967), p. 351, and reproduced in his *Studies in the Book of Esther* (Ktav, New York, 1982), pp. 521–528.

therefore of particular relevance to Esther studies. By means of cumulative evidence Moore establishes that Lagarde's A-text of Esther is not a recension of LXX but 'presupposes a Hebrew text very different at certain points from both the MT and the one presupposed by . . . the LXX'.[1] He thus shows that the Greek texts provide a primary tool for the Hebrew text of Esther.

3. *The Greek additions to the text of Esther*. The additions, to which reference has been made, were already part of the Greek text when Jerome was making his revised Latin translation at the end of the fourth century. The Vulgate, as his version came to be called, was based on the Hebrew as well as on the Greek text, and since these passages were not part of the Hebrew text he relegated them to a collection of deuterocanonical writings, which we know as the Apocrypha. There they can be read, but, separated off from the book to which they originally belonged, they make little sense, and are consequently largely ignored. They can be much better appreciated in the Jerusalem Bible, where the additional portions are easily recognized by italic printing, while at the same time occupying their appropriate place in the story.[2] They add 107 verses to the 167 of the Hebrew version, and form six major additions (not to mention small insertions), referred to by capital letters A to F according to the order in which they occur in the story, rather than that of LXX.

Rearranged as they are in the Jerusalem Bible, their contents may be summarized as follows:

A. This passage, seventeen verses long, forms an introduction, and relates two incidents, a dream of Mordecai and his discovery of the plot against the king. It is not considered to be all of a piece; the first ten verses show signs of a Semitic origin, and were in existence *c.* 114 BC, whereas verses 11–17, which were omitted by both Josephus and Old Latin, are likely to have been written in Greek as late as the second or third century AD.[3] The dream, with its apocalyptic features, has the effect of altering the focus of the story, so that it takes on cosmic importance. The struggle becomes one between the

[1]Carey A. Moore, *art. cit.*, p. 358.
[2]See also below, Appendix, pp. 119–126.
[3]For the details throughout the section on the Additions I am dependent on Carey A. Moore, 'On the Origins of the LXX Additions to the Book of Esther', *JBL* 92 (1973), pp. 382–393, which should be consulted for further information.

45

Jews and the rest of the world, and the dream is referred to as a 'vision of God's designs'.

B. The letter of Ahasuerus, inserted after chapter 3, together with E, the letter dictated by Mordecai, inserted in chapter 8, are both Greek compositions which were written before AD 94, because Josephus paraphrased them.

C. Inserted between chapters 4 and 5 are the prayers of Mordecai and Esther, which strengthen the religious emphasis of the book in Greek. Apart from verses 17–23, these prayers, which may have an Aramaic original, were written before AD 94.

D. This passage, chapter 15 in the Apocryphal Esther, describes her approach to the king, the focal point being verse 8: 'Then God changed the spirit of the king to gentleness. . .' Moore assesses that this was an original Greek composition written before AD 94.

F. This is the first of the additions in the Apocrypha. It relates Mordecai's interpretation of his dream and includes the colophon, or appended note, with details of the book's origin and date in its Greek version. Whereas we look for this information on the back of the title page of our printed books, in antiquity it was written at the end of a book; JB accordingly concludes with this verse, but because it was not strictly part of the story it is not printed in italics.

In Mordecai's interpretation of his dream the explanation differs considerably from the corresponding one in the so-called Lucianic text, at times contradicting it. By way of explanation of the discrepancy, Carey A. Moore postulates that A, the dream, and F originally circulated as a separate Semitic entity, independent of the Esther story, but, 'since in broad lines the dream could be adapted to Esther, it so was, even though some features of the dream were less appropriate than others'.[1] He judges that the Semitic *Vorlage* (the original Hebrew text) originated in Palestine, as did the colophon, and points out that the anti-Gentile attitude evident in the LXX version would be in keeping with that of Palestinian Jews of Roman times. As Moore mentions, the idea that all the nations were against the Jews, and therefore all the Jews were anti-Gentile, undoubtedly helps to explain why the book of Esther was never mentioned by the New Testament writers or by the

[1]Carey A. Moore, *art. cit.*, p. 389. He cites the colophon on p. 382.

Church Fathers, all of whom tended to use the LXX.[1] Leaders in the early Christian centuries were at pains to integrate Jewish and Gentile church members.

Most important of all the additions is the colophon, which, presuming that it is authentic (and there is no good reason to doubt its authenticity), gives the name of the translator as 'Lysimachus son of Ptolemy, a member of the Jerusalem community'. It was taken from Palestine to Egypt by 'Dositheus, who affirmed that he was a priest and Levite, and Ptolemy his son' 'in the fourth year of the reign of Ptolemy and Cleopatra', *i.e.* in 114 BC, if the Ptolemy and Cleopatra have been rightly identified. The book is referred to not as Esther but as 'the book of Purim', and the assertion of its authenticity, 'which they said was authentic', implies that other versions of the story were circulating, but that Lysimachus had worked from an authentic text.

It is not difficult to assess the reason for the church's relegation of these additions to less than canonical status; most weighty is the fact they do not feature in the Hebrew text, and indeed in some details even contradict the Hebrew, while others duplicate it. All the same it is intriguing to have the evidence of the Greek Esther on which to base an assessment of early objections to the shorter Hebrew version. It is also helpful to see how the different emphasis introduced by the extra material changed the character of the book.

4. *Other versions.* Of the many other versions the most important is that of Jerome into Latin, known as the Vulgate. At first Jerome intended to revise the current Latin translations, but discovered that he needed to start afresh from the Hebrew. The book of Esther he found to have been particularly corrupted, and he claims to have translated it afresh, word for word. Nevertheless it shows many minor deviations from MT, suggesting that he may well have had an independent text from which to work in Bethlehem. He is therefore a witness to the authoritative Hebrew text current in Palestine in the late fourth century AD.

The textual additions provide, in the main, evidence of tendencies to 'improve' on the shorter original, *i.* by documenting its authenticity and so making it more credible, and *ii.* by introducing into the story the name of God, not only in

---

[1]*Ibid.*, pp. 390f.

the new sections but also in the canonical portions.[1] While this latter change may on the surface appear to make the book more 'religious', it changes the author's emphasis and may distort the achievement of his purpose. We do well, therefore, to concentrate our attention on the story as it is recorded in our Bibles if we wish to understand what he was seeking to say. 'Commentators' do not always serve writers well, good though their intentions may be!

### VII. DATE OF WRITING

The earliest possible date for the book's first appearance is the reign of Ahasuerus, and since this is spoken of in 1:1 as though it had already become past history, it is most natural to suppose that Esther was written somewhat later in the Persian period, perhaps during the reign of the next king, Artaxerxes I (464–423 BC). There is little external evidence on which to base a judgment because there are no known references to the book in other literature. The author of Ecclesiasticus, Ben Sirach, did not include Mordecai or Esther among his heroes (Ecclus. 44–49), but he did not choose to mention Ezra either though he knew of Ezra's existence because he did include Nehemiah (Ecclus. 49:13). There is a reference to 'the day of Mordecai' in 2 Maccabees 15:36, but strictly speaking this proves only that when 2 Maccabees was written (probably about the middle of the first century BC) the festival of Purim was being observed. In any case the likelihood is that the translation of Esther into Greek had been undertaken earlier than this.[2]

Internal evidence is based mainly on the Hebrew of the book. Now that there is manuscript evidence from Qumran for the Hebrew language in the second century BC, it has become apparent to scholars that Esther belongs earlier than that. 'Esther's Hebrew has practically nothing in common with it; that alone would rule out a second-century date for Esther, and make a third-century date unlikely.'[3] This argues against attempts to date Esther in Maccabean times, and in any case the favourable relationship between the Jews and the

---

[1]'The most striking addition in the Greek text is God himself, the word or his name occurring over fifty times' (C. A. Moore, *Studies in the Book of Esther*, p. xxiv). Moore lists some of the more typical examples.
[2]See above, 'Text and Versions of Esther', pp. 43ff.
[3]The judgment of D. N. Freedman, quoted by C. A. Moore, *AB*, p. lvii.

Persian king makes the story unsuitable as the product of Palestine in the Maccabean period. The absence of words of Greek origin also argues against a date in the Greek empire, whereas the frequent occurrence of Persian words suggests a date during the Persian empire.[1]

Although certainty is impossible, the most likely period for the original Hebrew of Esther is the latter half of the fifth or the early fourth century BC. Not only does such a date accord well with the linguisitc evidence, but it also accounts for the accurate reflection of life at Susa in the time of Ahasuerus, and of the character of the king. The author had difficulty in finding acceptance with his Judean 'publishers', but in the long term his work became recognized and established.

## VIII. THE CANONICAL STATUS OF ESTHER

'All depends upon fate, even the Scriptures.' This Jewish maxim with which Jacob Hoshander opened his commentary on the book[2] is particularly applicable to the process by which the book of Esther came to be accepted as canonical. Not that all the steps in this mysterious process are ever clearly preserved, nor do we know exactly when the corpus of authoritative books which constitute our Old Testament became recognized for the first time. Though the word 'canon' was first used by Athanasius (d. AD 373), it is the opinion of S. Z. Leiman that the corpus of the Hebrew Scriptures was completed in Maccabean times.[3] Uncertainties abound, therefore, but in the case of the book of Esther there have been additional reasons for hesitation, examples of which continue to be voiced.

To begin with internal evidence, the book's Persian setting reflects a very different life-style from that of Judea and Jerusalem as depicted in Ezra-Nehemiah. Its alien culture and the absence of God's name provided sufficient reason for the book to be regarded with suspicion. It seemed, moreover, to have little religious significance. External evidence from Qumran seemed to support this judgment. Whereas every other book

---

[1]H. Striedl listed fifty-five, of which thirty-eight are personal names. *Cf.* C. A. Moore, *Studies in the Book of Esther*, pp. liv, lxxxi.

[2]*The Book of Esther in the Light of History* (Dropsie College, Philadelphia, 1923), p. 1; quoted by Berg, p. 1.

[3]S. Z. Leiman, *The Canonization of the Hebrew Scriptures* (Hamden: Archon Books, 1976).

of the Old Testament is represented among the documents found there, no fragment of Esther has been found. Though scholars have accounted for this in different ways, it has usually been assumed that for some reason the book was not important to the Qumran community, which in any case did not observe Purim and therefore scarcely needed the book which, superficially at least, seemed to be intended to authenticate this festival.[1] Whatever the reason for the absence of the book from Qumran, the fact indicates that in the second and first centuries BC Esther was not everywhere regarded as an indispensable part of Scripture.

Despite this negative evidence from Qumran, it seems from two other sources of information that the book was regarded as canonical by Jews of the first century AD. *i.* Josephus almost certainly included Esther among the twenty-two books he said constituted Scripture, for he related the contents as part of his history.[2] That he considered the events of the reign of Ahasuerus [Xerxes] as part of Scripture is clear: 'But as to the time from the death of Moses till the reign of Artaxerxes king of Persia, who reigned after Xerxes, the prophets, who were after Moses, wrote down what was done in their time in thirteen books.' He goes on to explain that since the time of Artaxerxes the record had not had the same degree of authority, because an exact succession of prophets had been lacking.[3] By implication he reckoned Mordecai to have been a prophet. *ii.* The Council of Jamnia (AD 90), traditionally associated with the fixing of the canon, almost certainly included Esther among the canonical books.

Among Jewish rabbis the book provoked extreme reactions. On the one hand there were those who considered the book

[1]One explanation which would account for the absence of Esther scrolls at Qumran is based on the suggestion that the texts found in the caves were not the library of the community but a collection of discarded sacred manuscripts. These could not be destroyed because they 'soiled the hands' and imparted ritual uncleanness, so instead they were committed to a 'genizah' or burying-place. Esther, which did not mention the name of God and was in any case read in the home at Purim, did not impart uncleanness and therefore did not need to be disposed of in a genizah. According to this theory of H. E. Del Medico, any defective scrolls of Esther would have been destroyed, and for this reason have not appeared amongst scriptures from the caves. The theory has not met with much support, but remains a possibility. *Cf.* Millar Burrows, *More Light on the Dead Sea Scrolls* (Secker and Warburg, 1958), pp. 15–19, 174–176.

[2]*Antiquities of the Jews* ii. 6.

[3]Flavius Josephus, *Against Apion* (tr. William Whiston) i. 8.

so highly that they rated it second only to the Law. Rabbi Simeon ben Lakish (*c.* AD 300) put Esther on the same level as the Law, while the medieval philosopher Maimonides (d. 1204) asserted that, 'when all the rest of the Old Testament passed away in the days of the coming of the Messiah, only Esther and the Law would remain'.[1] On the other hand there were those who pointed out that there was no sanction for Purim in the Law, that the book of Esther made no mention of God's name in any form, and that its vindictive spirit might antagonize Gentiles. The popularity of the Purim celebrations, intensified by persecutions, nevertheless secured the book's inclusion in the Jewish Scriptures, and skilful, somewhat forced, exegesis found ways round the objections. That Haman was an Agagite and therefore an Amalekite (1 Sa. 15:8), for example, made it possible for the rabbis to use Exodus 17:14 to prove that Purim was after all authorized in the Law!

If Jewish scholars were divided over Esther, so were the Church Fathers. C. A. Moore indicates on a map the main centres where Esther was regarded as canonical and those where it was not canonical.[2] It was omitted from the list of canonical books drawn up by Bishop Melito of Sardis in AD 170, but included by Origen, who wanted to base his Old Testament list on the twenty-one letters of the Hebrew alphabet, as Josephus had done. The judgments of Christian scholars as to the value of Esther have been closely bound up with their understanding of its intention. In so far as they thought it to be an authentication of the Jewish festival of Purim, they rejected it on the grounds that it promoted Jewish nationalism and encouraged genocide. It is worth remembering that these churches had the book in its Greek translation, with the Additions, which put a particular slant on its message. Even so the Council of Carthage in AD 397 gave the book its secure place in the Christian Scriptures which it has held ever since.

The separation of the 'Additions' and their relegation to the Apocrypha at the time of the Reformation permitted the original Hebrew book to be read and interpreted afresh. Even so there has been no lack of detractors, who would recommend its exclusion from the canon. The most famous of these is Martin Luther, who in his *Table Talk* said of 2 Maccabees

---

[1] *Cf.* G. F. Moore, *Judaism* I (Cambridge, 1946), p. 245.
[2] *AB*, pp. xxvif.

and of Esther, 'I wish that they did not exist at all; for they Judaize too much and have much heathen perverseness'.[1] In recent years there has even been a protest from a Jewish writer, who expressed the opinion that both Purim and the book of Esther were unworthy of their nation.[2] But despite such derogatory judgments the book is well established as part of Scripture and is not likely to be rejected.

For the Jewish people it has been the ground for hope in their ongoing sufferings. They have looked for vindication and they have not been disappointed. Christians for their part cannot dismiss the Jews from their reckoning. The providence of God continues to be traceable in their survival and in the establishment of their state of Israel, and it behoves the Christian to stand in awe (Rom. 11:20). Though powerful voices have been raised against it, the book goes on making its contribution to Scripture, the story of its vicissitudes in connection with the canon reinforcing the story of Esther, that chance comes to us from the hand of God.

[1]Martin Luther, *Table Talk*, xxii.
[2]Shalom ben Chorin, *Kritik des Estherbuches: Eine theologische Streitschrift* (Jerusalem, 1938), p. 5. quoted by B. W. Anderson, 'The Place of the Book of Esther in the Christian Bible' in *Journal of Religion* 30 (1950), p. 34.

# ANALYSIS

I. THE SCENE IS SET (1:1–22)
   a. Persian splendour (1:1–9)
   b. The king defied (1:10–12)
   c. The king avenged (1:13–22)

II. ESTHER IS CHOSEN QUEEN (2:1–18)
   a. Regrets not permitted (2:1–4)
   b. Esther introduced (2:5–11)
   c. Esther becomes queen (2:12–18)

III. A PLOT IS DISCLOSED (2:19–23)

IV. HAMAN TAKES VENGEANCE ON THE JEWS (3:1–15)
   a. Haman's promotion (3:1–6)
   b. The casting of lots (3:7–11)
   c. The edict sent out (3:12–15)

V. ESTHER AGREES TO INTERCEDE (4:1–17)
   a. Mordecai's passionate outburst (4:1–3)
   b. Esther takes the lead (4:4–17)

VI. ESTHER FINDS FAVOUR (5:1–14)
   a. Esther's petition (5:1–8)
   b. Haman's vexation (5:9–14)

VII. HAMAN INADVERTENTLY PROMOTES MORDECAI (6:1–13)
   a. The king's bedtime book (6:1–3)
   b. Haman's humiliation (6:4–13)

VIII. QUEEN ESTHER'S SECOND FEAST (6:14 – 7:10)

IX. AHASUERUS TURNS THE TABLES (8:1–17)
   a. Vacant places filled (8:1–2)
   b. Reversal of the edict (8:3–14)
   c. The popularity of the Jews (8:15–17)

## ANALYSIS

# COMMENTARY

## I. THE SCENE IS SET (1:1–22)

### a. Persian spendour (1:1–9)

With an economy of words the story-teller transports his listeners to a fabulous oriental world, and to a time when the Persian empire was still young. For the majority of people in western Asia, then as now, life was hard and food none too plentiful. While labourers received barely enough to live on, even though they were producing works of art that are still unsurpassed, life at court was extravagant beyond imagining. The more lavish the king's hospitality, the greater his claim to supremacy. Strangely to our ears no protest was even hinted at. Nevertheless Jewish listeners, brought up on the Prophets, were sure to be making their own observations, and silently assessing the injustice of a system that created so great a gulf between rich and poor.

**1.** In Hebrew the book begins with a formula, translated in AV, RV 'now it came to pass', but omitted in RSV. It regularly introduces the history books of the Bible, whose story continues what has gone before, and in view of the fact that Greek versions of *Esther* have two paragraphs at the beginning which do not appear in the Hebrew (see Appendix, **A.**, pp. 119f., below),this connecting formula could reflect the existence of a longer original in Hebrew also. Another deduction is that the writer wanted to suggest that his book belonged to the class of historical literature.[1] But the same opening is used in the books of Ezekiel and Jonah, so neither argument carries much weight. It was a conventional introductory expression.

*Ahasuerus*, in Greek Xerxes, is the Persian king mentioned in Ezra 4:6 who reigned 486–465 BC. Strangely the Greek versions have instead the name Artaxerxes.[2] Ahasuerus is known in the West as the king who took on the Greeks and

---

[1] *ICC*, p. 121.    [2] On the identity of the king see Introduction, pp. 17ff.

who was twice humiliated by them (in 480 and 479 BC), but he was also a great builder, who completed and improved upon the great palaces which his father, Darius, had begun, and he consolidated the empire *from India to Ethiopia*. By *India* is meant the area drained by the Indus river, now Pakistan, not peninsular India. Attracted by the gold dust carried by the rivers of the Indus plain, Darius had conquered it before 513 BC.[1] *Ethiopia* (Heb. *Kûš*) was the country south of Egypt, now part of the Northern Sudan, not modern Ethiopia. Early in his reign, Darius had reconquered Egypt, and took advantage of work already begun to complete a canal from the Mediterranean to the Red Sea. The commercial and military advantages were obvious.[2] *One hundred and twenty-seven provinces*. The primary divisions of the empire were the satrapies, of which there were never more than thirty-one. By quoting the higher number of provinces, the domain of the king is made as impressive as possible.

**2.** *Sat on his royal throne*. Persian kings are often portrayed in great splendour, sitting on straight-backed thrones, surrounded by attendants. In this verse more is implied, for there had been obstacles in the way of a peaceful accession, and he had had to quell risings in Egypt and Babylon.[3] The word *royal* (Heb. *malkûtô*), literally 'of his kingdom', is found mainly in the later books of the Old Testament, 1 and 2 Chronicles, Esther, Daniel and Ezra. *Susa* had been the capital of Elam, and was taken over by the Persian monarchs and rebuilt. The word translated *capital* (Heb. *bîrâ*) is a late loan-word with equivalents in Assyrian and Persian, and means 'acropolis', the strongly fortified palace complex within the city, and elevated above it in this case by 120 feet. Everything was designed to exalt the importance of the king as well as to guard his person.

**3.** *In the third year of his reign* would be 483 BC, by which time, having settled the empire and completed the building needed at Susa, he was ready to celebrate by giving a *banquet*. The Hebrew word is cognate with the verb 'to drink' and so implied that there would be an ample supply of wine. To the banquet were invited his officials (EVV *princes* is misleading). These were people appointed rather than born to office, and the same word *śārîm* is translated 'governors' later in this verse. *Servants*, literally 'slaves', means courtiers close to the

---

[1] *HPE*, pp. 144f.   [2] *HPE*, pp. 145–147   [3] *HPE*, pp. 234–237.

king (*cf.* 3:2; 4:11; 5:11), like Nehemiah a little later (Ne. 1:11). *The army chiefs* (lit. 'army') is an amendment made in the cause of good sense, for it is assumed that this must be the meaning. The picked troops numbered 14,000 and the bodyguard were the Ten Thousand Immortals.[1] *Persia and Media* is the reverse of the order familiar from Daniel 5:28; 6:8ff.; 8:20. The two nations were closely related racially; in the period up to 550 the Medes were dominant, whereas after 550, when Cyrus began to come to power, the Persians took the lead. It was natural that the Persian king put his nation first. *Nobles* (Heb. *part<sup>e</sup>mîm*) is a Persian loan-word, which occurs also in Daniel 1:3. There are Median and Persian nobles depicted in relief on the stairs of the king's Audience Hall at Persepolis.[2]

**4.** Ahasuerus had inherited from his father Darius unprecedented wealth, the lavish new buildings at Susa and gold in plenty, together with luxury goods, largely provided by taxation and tribute. For 180 days the royal treasures were on display, and while so many influential people were at the court it would have been a good opportunity to plan the Greek campaign. As in the case of Hezekiah and the Babylonian envoys (2 Ki. 20:12–19; Is. 39:1–8), resources were liable to be translated into military terms. Strictly as it is written the text appears to say that the feast lasted all of six months, 'an incredibly long time for the King and all the officials of the empire to spend in drinking', as Paton remarks.[3] Probably we are meant to understand that, having first mentioned the banquet, the writer explains the circumstances before returning to his main topic.

**5.** The banquet then was the culmination of the festivities. Many would consider even seven days too long a time for such a carousal, but the intention is to conjure up an impression (not without irony) of the unlimited resources of the king, who could invite *all the people in Susa*'s acropolis (*cf.* comment on v. 2, above), that is, the king's entourage, officials and visitors, *both great and small*, of all ranks. It was to be held out of doors, in the court of the garden of the king's *palace*, better 'pavilion' (Heb. *bîtan; cf.* 7:7), 'a small luxury structure, an

---

[1]*HPE*, pp. 237–247. Plate XXXI shows the Immortals depicted at Persepolis.
[2]*IBD* III, p. 1195, shows the stairway. The nobles can be seen in *HPE*, Plate XXVII.
[3]*ICC*, p. 131.

independent architectural unit for the use of the king or the heir apparent ... an open structure, probably a colonnaded open hall'.[1] Susa was intensely hot in summer, when any slight breeze would be welcome.

**6.** An impressionistic description conjures up an exotic picture of the setting. An unconnected noun, 'white stuff', makes an unexpected opening to the verse; rsv supplies 'there were', and the 'stuff' is presumed to be in the form of curtains; so with the *blue* or violet material, draped and caught back with linen cords. White and violet were the royal colours, and therefore appropriate for the occasion. The contrasting colours of marble columns, gold and silver couches and the ornamental pattern of the mosaic floor enhanced the royal splendour. The Persian custom of reclining at table had already made its appearance in Israel at the time of Amos (Am. 6:4), and was to become the accepted practice in New Testament times.

**7.** Persian goblets of gold were more like drinking-horns in shape and capacity, individually designed and beautifully decorated.[2]

**8.** This verse has proved to be problematic for translators and commentators. On the one hand drinking was 'according to the law' (Heb. *kaddāt*), while on the other hand each one (lit. 'man and man') was free to do as he desired. Much depends on the degree of importance attached to the word *dāt*. According to Paton this Persian word comes nineteen times in the book, always with reference to a royal decree.[3] The 'law' referred to has therefore been taken to be one of those important, unalterable laws of the Medes and Persians. According to Herodotus and Xenophon there was a law that whenever the king drank, everyone drank. Josephus, however, retelling the story, said, 'He [the king] also gave order to the servants, that they should not force them to drink, by bringing them wine continually, as is the practice of the Persians, but to permit every one of the guests to enjoy himself according

---

[1]A. L. Oppenheim, 'On Royal Gardens in Mesopotamia', *JNES* 24 (1965), pp. 330ff.; formal, ornamental gardens were well attested in Egypt, while Nebuchadrezzar chose landscaping to look like mountains, with trees of all kinds (p. 332).

[2]For examples see *AB*, Plate 6, and the British Museum. One drinking-horn (bm 124081) in parcel-gilt silver, 25cm high, with the butt in the form of a crouching griffin, dates from the Achaemenid Persian period, 5th century bc.

[3]*ICC*, p. 146.

to his own inclination.'[1] Josephus, however, was following LXX, which inserted a negative and so completely changed the sense of the second clause, as it stands in Hebrew and standard English versions. His contribution therefore does not help.

It may be that interpreters have been over-influenced by the word *dāt*, which might on occasions have had the force of 'order' rather than 'decree', thus giving good sense, as in NIV, 'By the king's command each guest was allowed to drink in his own way, for the king instructed all the wine stewards to serve each man what he wished.' Mention should be made of one further contribution to the meaning of this verse. The word *kaddāt* may mean 'flagons', in which case there would be no mention of a decree, and the meaning would be 'the drinking was by flagons without restraint'.[2] Probably NIV represents the best solution so far to the problem.

Hidden in translation, but obvious in the Hebrew text, are occasional nuances of word-play. There is, for example, repetition of the word *rab*, 'much, many', translated in verse 7 'bounty' and hidden in the English 'all' in verse 8. This king was lavish in stocking his wine-cellar and in engaging servants.

**9.** Meanwhile another similar banquet was being held for the women, presided over by the queen. Some writers are of the opinion that a total of three banquets are mentioned in these few verses, so emphasizing this as one of the favourite themes of the author.[3] Undoubtedly the story involves several feasts, so that he could hardly avoid making them a feature of his book. It does not seem to have been usual to entertain the women separately in Persian custom; indeed Esther herself entertained the king and Haman to a feast. The size of the guest-list may have made some division of numbers necessary, or we may be intended to infer that the excesses of the banquet would have offended the sensibilities of these ladies.

The name *Vashti* is puzzling because, according to Herodotus, the queen's name was Amestris, daughter of Otanes, who had supported Darius in his bid for the throne in 522 BC,

[1] *Antiquities of the Jews* xi. 6.1.

[2] John Gray, *The Legacy of Canaan*, VTS V (Leiden, 1956), p. 226; quoted by Moore, *AB*, p. 8.

[3] Three banquets result from separating that in v.3 from the one in v.5, on the ground that the latter was intended for the common people, but if *bîrâ* should be translated 'acropolis' as we have argued, the guests did not come from the main city across the river, called *hāʿîr* in 3:15b. S. B. Berg accepts that both feasts were for the acropolis, but lays stress on what she sees as different guest-lists (Berg, p. 32).

but it is possible that he had other queens, whose names do not happen to have come to light, or that she had alternative names. The name Vashti, which is spelt in seven different ways in as many versions, has been associated with Persian words meaning 'best' or 'the beloved', 'the desired one', a lovely name by which to be known.[1]

## b. The king defied (1:10–12)

The great king who ruled the known world and enjoyed unlimited resources and prestige was nevertheless vulnerable. This incident raised the question as to who had the last word at home.

**10.** After a week of indulgence the king's heart may well have been *merry*. The Hebrew word *ṭôḇ*, 'good', can mean anything from 'cheerful' to 'drunk'; the context decides (*cf.* 1 Sa. 25:36 and 1 Ki. 8:66 for contrasting interpretations of the same idiom). Ahasuerus is hardly likely to have been entirely sober. The seven names vary very much in form in the Versions and are unconfirmed from external sources, though *Mehuman* is a Hebraized form of an Old Persian word (it means 'trusty') and the last, *Carkas*, appears in the *Persepolis Treasury Tablets*. In general the names support a Persian origin and lack evidence of Greek influence. The Hebrew word *sārîs*, 'eunuch', implies both 'chief officer' and 'castrate' in this context, for these seven men were permitted access to the royal harem; but it could mean merely 'officer', as in the case of Potiphar (Gn. 37:36), who was of course a married man.

**11–12.** Regarding Vashti as his most precious treasure, the king wanted to bring his great exhibition to a climax by displaying her beauty. Her impertinence in refusing to appear, so humiliating the king in front of all the leaders of the realm, was predictably dangerous on her part. Variant readings and additions in the early Jewish texts attempt to explain her disobedience. Either she was required to appear naked, or she had some disfigurement, both of which eventualities would have made her refusal understandable in Jewish eyes, or she was openly flouting her husband's authority, considering that his authority had proper limits. The omission of a reason strengthens the tension of the story by implying that Vashti had no rights in relation to her husband, and therefore reasons

[1]*AB*, p. 8. See also p. xlii.

were irrelevant. Did the writer have some sympathy for Vashti and expect to evoke pity in his readers? He seems to have succeeded in doing so. The burning resentment of the king was certain to find expression, to Vashti's disadvantage.

### c. The king avenged (1:13–22)

**13–14.** Royal advisers, *wise men*, were a traditional institution; such were consulted by the Pharaoh (Gn. 41:8) and Daniel was among their number at Babylon in the time of Nebuchadrezzar. The *times* were strictly propitious occasions for action according to the stars, but here the expression seems to mean 'the right course to follow' (*cf.* 1 Ch. 12:32). The long parenthesis is typical of the style of the writer (a shorter example occurred in 1:1). The king habitually consulted his specialists in *law* and *judgment* (Heb. *dāt* and *dîn*): the alliteration evidently appealed to the author, for the stock phrase did not exactly suit the need. There is not likely to have been a precedent for such a situation. A preference for the number seven is becoming apparent (*cf.* v.10).

The *men next to him* were the most trusted of the wise men, selected and privileged to *see the king's face*, *i.e.* talk to him personally, a rare prerogative. These seven were the nearest to peers in his realm. There is little to say about their names, although some of their spellings differ considerably in the Versions, but like the names in verse 10 they appear to be probable Persian forms.[1] The first, *Carshena*, is found at Persepolis in the Fortification Tablets. Artaxerxes also had seven counsellors (Ezr. 7:14).

**15.** The writer now picks up from before the parenthesis in verse 13. If the king was at a loss to know how to proceed, his request for a directive *according to the law* avoided any admission of inadequacy.

**16.** An inner cabinet of king, princes and advisers consulted together. Memucan proved his worth. It was astute of him to take the heat out of the king's personal resentment by setting the incident in a wider context. It was also a clever move to make the most of the fact that he had an all-male gathering before him. By gaining their support he could make capital out of an unfortunate setback at the expense of the queen.

**17.** The argument of Memucan may have commended itself

---

[1] *AB*, p. xliii, sets out the variant forms of the names.

to the men present, but it took little account of female psychology. Women do not as a rule support one another as readily as men in taking concerted action.

**18–20**. The thought of female jokes and gossip at male expense provided sufficient incentive for a new royal decree, though how it could be enforced is not considered. For his part the king would include in the decree a bill of divorce, banishing Vashti from him, and the example would intimidate any wives who dared to defy their husbands. The very proclamation of the law would achieve the desired submission!

The omission of the title 'Queen' before Vashti's name from this point on is noteworthy. *Another who is better than she* anticipates the way the story will develop. In view of the regal isolation of the king, the queen's influence was potentially very great, and the next occupant of that *royal position* was to exploit her power to the full. Just how great her power was is explored in the course of the story. Vashti forfeited her influence by breaking the unspoken rule that it should be wielded in private. There is an appropriateness about her punishment. If she will not come when summoned, let her not come ever again. G. A. F. Knight sees Memucan as typical of those who delight to get other people into trouble, and bring destruction upon innocent lives.[1]

**21–22**. Memucan's appeal to male self-interest won the support of both king and princes. By depicting the king dispatching his edict without so much as a further thought, the author indirectly comments on the whimsical way laws were made in a land which made so much of law and judgment (*cf.* v. 13). L. B. Paton goes into some detail over the many languages spoken in the Persian empire at the time, and says he would have expected one edict in Aramaic, the official international language, to be issued.[2] Yet, given a great international gathering, there would have been no shortage of translators, or of messengers, though the postal system of which Herodotus wrote[3] could also have carried the edicts. Yet the contents could scarcely fail to strike the recipients as ludicrous, for every husband was expected to rule in his own home. *Speak according to the language of his people*, omitted from the Greek, is unexpected. Early Jewish commentators read this in the light of Nehemiah 13:23f., as a directive that husbands with foreign wives should continue to speak their

---

[1]*TBC*, p. 29.　　[2]*ICC*, pp. 161f.　　[3]Herodotus, *The Histories* viii. 98.

own language, but that hardly fits this context. AV and RV take liberties with the Hebrew without gaining appreciably in meaning. A slight emendation gives the reading 'Say whatever suited him', and this certainly makes good sense.[1] The Hebrew would be explained, however, if Ahasuerus was taking a leaf out of Cyrus's book and encouraging the development of minority cultures.[2] The stress on translation of the edict into the languages of the peoples would support this.

In this introduction to the Persian court the external trappings and the human scene are depicted in all their bizarre splendour. As compared with modern story-telling this presentation is entirely objective; the author avoids comment, attempts no character study, no psychological interpretation, passes no judgment. The reader is left to make his own deductions, and no doubt the original Jewish members of the Diaspora still living under alien rule were quick to do so.

For us who live in a very different age it would be easy to miss the subtle irony and humour, obvious to the original readers. There are several ironical nuances, but the most obvious is the contrast between King Ahasuerus at the beginning of the chapter, when he is the world's greatest monarch, rich and powerful, aloof yet generous, and that same king by the end of the chapter, attempting to maintain his dignity despite the defiance of his wife. This law-maker of the Persians and Medes, whose law could not be altered, was prepared to pass an edict framed in a moment of pique, when he was not even sober. The counsellors represented by Memucan were clever but hardly wise; the decree promulgated according to their advice made the king look a fool in the eyes of his subjects, and he may even have regretted the banishment of Vashti in his better moments (2:1). Is this the measure of the king who reigned over the world, and had the future of all in his power? The security and confidence of the author, who could comment in this way on the highest ruler in the contemporary world as well as on the court and its intrigues, is striking, and witnesses in a totally unconscious way to the efficacy of faith in the living God. This writer knew nothing of an identity crisis, nor was he dismayed by the inadequacies of human government of which he was so aware, because of

---

[1]*AB*, p. 12, following a suggestion of Hitzig; *cf. ICC*, p. 162.

[2]From surviving texts we know that Cyrus restored the sanctuaries of subject peoples, and returned exiles (not only those of Judah) to their homes (*ANET*, p. 316).

the overarching government of the one he worshipped but did not name.

## II. ESTHER IS CHOSEN QUEEN (2:1–18)

### a. Regrets not permitted (2:1–4)

Though *after these things* is a general indication of time, the king's change of mood suggests a shorter rather than a longer period before his wrath *abated*. This verb (Heb. *šākak*), which occurs only five times altogether in the Old Testament, is found again in 7:10, so tending to link these incidents (*cf.* Introduction, pp. 30f.). That Ahasuerus *remembered* Vashti implies some uneasiness over the whole incident, but the king was trapped by his own legislation *decreed against* her. The verb (Heb. *gāzar*) meant 'cut, divide' and is an Aramaism in the sense of 'decree'.

The servants who waited on the king took their cue and urged the implementation of Memucan's suggestion. There was considerable enthusiasm for the task of finding and bringing to Susa all the most attractive girls of the kingdom, but this was more than a beauty contest, and, as I have written elsewhere,[1] from the point of view of the girls involved, no enviable fate, despite the glamour of travel and the possibility of becoming the royal spouse. It was customary to put a eunuch in charge of 'the house of the women', a most responsible post. The name *Hegai* occurs in its Greek form Hegias in Herodotus as an officer of Xerxes.[2]

Likenesses between *The Thousand and One Nights* and this incident in the book of Esther are often drawn, but it is impossible to ascertain the date of the Arabian legend and therefore to make any significant comparison. H. Ringgren argues that the 'beauty contest' in a royal context is 'a standing motif, perhaps a wandering motif'. 'At least it can be said that this book does not present something unheard of in the milieu in which it was formed.'[3]

---

[1]*NBC*, p. 415.    [2]*The Histories* ix. 34.
[3]H. Ringgren, 'Skonhetsavlingen i Esters bok', *SEÅ* 46 (1981), pp. 69–73, as summarized in *OTA* (1982), 5, p. 60.

### b. Esther introduced (2:5–11)

A flash-back to the time of the deportation of the Jews from Jerusalem in 597 BC interrupts the story to introduce two key people, indispensable for the plot.

**5–6.** 'A man of Judah there was. . .' A new character is signalled by the inversion of the usual word order. As the text goes on to say, Mordecai was of the tribe of Benjamin; the name Judah had by this time become generalized to mean 'Jew' as well as conveying tribal significance. The names in Mordecai's genealogy are probably those well known from the family of King Saul: *Kish*, his ancestor (1 Sa. 9:1; 14:51; 1 Ch. 8:33), and *Shimei*, his relative, who out of fierce loyalty for Saul cursed David (2 Sa. 16:5). If so, such ancestors prove Mordecai to have a claim to royal blood; but be that as it may, he is a member of God's chosen people, who inherited the promises (*e.g.* Is. 62:1–2). For that reason some special fulfilment of the promises is expected. *Who had been carried away.* It is not clear to which name the 'who' refers; grammatically Mordecai is indicated, but this would make both him and Esther too old by 480 BC. There are other examples in Scripture of a telescoping of generations, in keeping with an awareness of family solidarity (*cf.* Gn. 46:27; Heb. 7:10).

The name *Mordecai*, like the names given to Daniel and his friends (Dn. 1:7), derives from a name current in Babylon. It incorporates Marduk, the name of the state god of Babylon, and may be a Hebrew version of the common name Marduka.[1] It occurs in several forms in the treasury tablets found at Persepolis; it appears as *Mrdk* in a fifth-century Aramaic document, and in an undated text, coming probably from either the last years of Darius I or the early years of Xerxes I, where mention is made of a man named Marduka, who served as an accountant on an inspection tour from Susa.[2] *Jeconiah*, also known as Coniah (Je. 22:24–30) and as Jehoiachin (2 Ki. 24:6–17), was Judah's king in 597 and so was deported by Nebuchadrezzar to Babylon, there to become the hope of the exiles (2 Ki. 25:27–30). That the family of Mordecai was taken with Jehoiachin probably means that he was among the nobility (2 Ki. 24:12).

**7.** *Hadassah* is the Hebrew name of the heroine and means

[1] *IBD* II, p. 1024.
[2] C. A. Moore, 'Archaeology and the Book of Esther', *BA* 38 (1975), p. 74. He refers to A. Ungnad, *ZAW* 58 (1940/41), p. 244.

'myrtle'.[1] In prophetic symbolism the myrtle would replace the briars and thorns of the desert, so depicting the Lord's forgiveness and acceptance of his people (Is. 41:19; 55:13; *cf.* Zc. 1:8). Myrtle branches are still carried in procession at the feast of Tabernacles, and signify peace and thanksgiving. The Persian equivalent, *Esther*, 'star' (*cf.* Stella), picks up the sound of the Hebrew, and suggests the star-like flowers of the myrtle. It comes from the same root as the Babylonian Ishtar, the goddess who corresponds to Venus in Roman worship.

Mordecai had adopted his orphaned cousin and brought her up. She was *beautiful* and *lovely*. The Hebrew is more specific, 'beautiful in form and lovely to look at', 'lovely in form and features' (NIV). The verb translated 'adopt' is *lāqaḥ*, 'take', which is used in a more general sense in the next verse.

The practice of adoption was sufficently well known in Israel to provide a model for the relationship between the Lord and his people (*cf.* Ex. 4:22; 2 Sa. 7:14; Pss. 2:7-8; 89:27-28; Je. 3:19; 31:9), yet there are no laws in the Pentateuch governing adoption, and relatively few examples of its practice (but *cf.* Gn. 15:3; 48:5; Is. 1:2-3; Ho. 11:1). This example in Esther suggests that adoption within the family was preferred, and this is in keeping with Near Eastern custom.[2]

**8.** The parenthesis over, the writer resumes the story he began in verses 1-4. The vague statement *many maidens* has provoked guesses as to a likely number. According to Josephus there were four hundred, but Paton, estimating at the rate of a different girl per night for four years (16; *cf.* 1:3), arrives at 1,460.[3] No restriction seems to have been placed on numbers. As in the case of the banquet everything was possible at the Persian court. *Esther also was taken*, as she had been taken into Mordecai's care. C. A. Moore is right, of course, that the verb does not suggest 'anything unpleasant', but it is impossible to know whether she went without reluctance. It is questionable whether any woman could exercise the right of choice in the face of a royal order.

**9.** The immediate approval of Hegai would be reassuring. He was charmed by Esther and she received favour (*cf.* 'God gave Daniel favour', Dn. 1:9), as she was later to receive

[1] *IBD* III, pp. 1238, 1240
[2] Josephus, *Antiquities of the Jews* xi. 6.2. *Cf. ICC*, pp. 172f.
[3] For further information see *IBD* I, article 'Adoption', p. 17; S. M. Paul, 'Adoption formulae', *Maarav* 2 (1980), pp. 173-185.

favour in the eyes of the king (5:2). It is instructive to note the use of the covenant word *favour* (Heb. *ḥeseḏ*) in these secular contexts. The theological restraint of the author of Esther as contrasted with Daniel 1:9, though under-expressing the sense of God's leading, may yet imply it. Interpreters have wondered why, unlike Daniel and his friends, Esther, as a loyal member of the Jewish race, made no protest about eating the unclean food of the Gentiles. Her situation was different from that of Daniel in that, as a potential wife of the king, she had to expect to be his sole companion at table, and would be committed to sharing his meals. Her mission was also different, and her integrity expresses itself in its own appropriate way as the story unfolds.[1]

Hegai did all he could to speed the preparations, and by giving her seven attendants and the best apartments he seems to have singled Esther out as the favourite for the queenly succession.

**10.** Esther's ability to keep her own counsel was one of the signs of wisdom (Pr. 13:3), as was her obedience to Mordecai's instructions (Pr. 13:1). He ruled his household! She was a person of discretion and not just a pretty face; indeed discretion enhances beauty. According to Herodotus Ahasuerus should have been looking for a wife in the restricted circle of the families of his six confederates.[2] The fact that he asked no questions meant that Esther deceived no-one by keeping her lineage to herself.

**11.** Mordecai's separation from Esther was complete; hence his concern to obtain news of her. How he did so is unimportant for the story, and is therefore left to the imagination, but servants love to prove that they are in the know. More significant is the affection which took him daily to the courtyard of her part of the palace, to glean information about her.

### c. Esther becomes queen (2:12–18)

The elaborate beauty treatment to which each candidate had to submit is now set out in some detail.

**12–14.** These verses highlight the inhumanity of polygamy. The twelve months of beauty treatment provided 'marriage preparation', but the sad part was that for the majority what

[1]See *Daniel* (*TOTC*), p. 83, on 1:9.
[2]Herodotus, *The Histories* iii. 84.

awaited them was more like widowhood than marriage. Though each girl in turn moved from the house of Hegai to that of Shaashgaz once she had become a concubine, there was no guarantee that the king would remember her by name and call for her even once more. Quite apart from the emotional deprivation this entailed, were not young men in their villages deprived of wives by the king's greed? The prestige of living in the royal palace was small compensation for the king's neglect, though girls with a passion for luxury could no doubt indulge it to the full.

Some commentators have seen humour in the importance given to beauty and cosmetics. B. W. Jones, for example, calls the twelve-month beauty treatment "conspicuous consumption" in the extreme'.[1] Persia and India, together with Arabia, were famous for their aromatic perfumes which they exported from time immemorial, so it is not surprising that full use of them was made at the royal harem.[2] Even today vestiges of ancient customs connected with preparation of the bride for her wedding survive in parts of Iran and north India. These include ritual cleansing at the communal bathhouse, the plucking of eyebrows and removal of body hair, and the painting of hands and feet with henna, in addition to facial make-up.[3] Application of beautifying paste over several months could be expected to lighten the colour of the skin and remove spots and blemishes, much as face-packs are used today. Oil of *myrrh* was valued for its sweet perfume (Ps. 45:8; Pr. 7:17). There can be no doubt about the seriousness with which all this beauty treatment was applied.

A further contribution to the subject by W. F. Albright has drawn attention to the use of cosmetic burners during the fifth century BC in South Arabia, Palestine and Mesopotamia. On the basis of a study of inscriptions on such burners he suggests that the fragrant spices mentioned here were used in fumi-

---

[1] B. W. Jones, 'Two misconceptions re the Book of Esther', *CBQ* 39 (1977), p. 175. *Cf.* T. H. Gaster, 'Esther 1:22', *JBL* 69 (1950), p. 81; and Berg, p. 28.

[2] *Cf.* Athalya Brenner, 'Aromatics and Perfumes in the Song of Songs', *JSOT* 25 (1983), pp. 75–81.

[3] In India a beautifying paste is made from flour, mustard oil and tumeric; saffron too may have been used, though now it is very expensive. In Bengal sandalwood is used to form a paste and perfumed water for bathing. In some areas the paste is applied all over the body for several days before the marriage. Since one intention is to lighten the skin, sunbathing is considered a strange practice.

gation, 'which would have both hygenic and therapeutic value'.[1]

**15.** Only now is Esther referred to by her full name, Bath-Abihail (Bath meaning 'daughter of '), *the uncle of Mordecai, who had adopted her.* The offer of all kinds of adornment meant that prospective queens revealed by the choice they made whether they had good judgment and artistic sense, or whether they were interested only in enriching themselves. Esther was prepared to be guided by Hegai, who no doubt knew what was in keeping with the king's preferences.

**16–18.** Four years had passed since the king by his edict had banished Vashti (*cf.* 1:3). The tenth month, *Tebeth*, 'mud', was mid-winter, a cold, wet period even in Susa. Despite the weather the king 'loved' Esther *more than all the women* he had so far seen, and waited no longer before declaring her queen. Thus she gained grace and favour in the eyes of the king, as she had done with Hegai and others (2:9,15). The royal *crown* (Heb. *keṭer*), which may be a Persian loan-word, is related to the Hebrew verb 'to surround', hence 'circlet'. The choice of the new queen called for another banquet, this time in honour of Esther. *A remission of taxes*, unlikely as it seems to the western reader, is well attested in ancient Persia.[2] An extra day's holiday, on the other hand, is associated in our minds with a royal marriage. The question is, which reading is correct, the text or the margin of RSV? The Hebrew is literally 'a causing to rest', an idiom which requires the translator to interpret the sense. Greek translators thought it meant 'release for prisoners', which is another possibility, but in the absence of firm evidence for any meaning except the first, the RSV text must stand. The *gifts* of the king on this occasion would probably be portions of food (*cf.* Gn. 43:34; Je. 40:5 where the same word *maś'ēt* occurs and the context supplies the meaning), and so all the population, and not merely the rich and influential, had cause for rejoicing.

---

[1]'The Lachish Cosmetic Burner and Esther 2:12' in *A Light unto My Path: Old Testament Studies in Honor of Jacob M. Myers*, edited by H. N. Bream, R. D. Heim and C. A. Moore (Temple University Press, Philadelphia, 1974), p. 31. The article is reprinted in C. A. Moore, *Studies in the Book of Esther*, pp. 361–368.

[2]Herodotus, *The Histories* iii. 67. Pseudo-Smerdis, directly he came to the throne, proclaimed 'a three years' remission of taxes and military service'.

## III. A PLOT DISCLOSED (2:19–23)

The opening sentence of this section has caused problems, because both its meaning and its significance to the author are unclear. The difficulties centre, *i.* on the Hebrew word translated *the second time* (Heb. *šēnît*), for there had not apparently been such a gathering before, and there are almost as many explanations as commentators.[1] The meaning may have eluded some of the earliest translators into Greek and Latin, for they omitted the opening clause. Perhaps the emendation, small in the Hebrew consonantal text, from *šēnît* to *šōnôt*, should be favourably considered.[2] The meaning would then be 'when various virgins were being gathered together', that is, recapitulating verse 8. But this has to be weighed up in the light of the meaning of the second clause. *ii.* In view of the fact that Mordecai was regularly to be found sitting at the king's gate (2:21; 3:2; 5:9, 13; 6:10, 12), why does the author make so much of the point? Have two separate motifs concerning Esther and Mordecai independently been incompletely put together?[3] The implication of the phrase *sitting in the king's gate* has been taken up by Gordis, who claims that it is not 'a meaningless tag in any of its five occurrences in the book'.[4] He points out that, throughout the ancient Near East, 'the gate' was the area where justice was dispensed, and that, while the litigant stood, the king or his appointed official 'sat' (*cf.* Pr. 31:23, rsv). The turn of phrase in 19b thus takes on concrete significance, and Gordis makes the feasible suggestion that Esther, when she became queen, had Mordecai appointed a magistrate or judge, 'a lesser position in the elaborate hierarchy of Persian officials', and that she accomplished this without delay, 'before the final ceremonial parade that concluded the coronation festivities'.[5] If this is right reasoning 2:19–20 does not merely recapitulate 2:8–10, but adds an important incident in the development of the plot. Mordecai is now in a position to overhear what is being said by palace officials (21) and to have access to the royal courts

[1] *Cf.* the comprehensive summary of suggestions in *ICC*, pp. 186–188.
[2] This was suggested in 1908 by L. B. Paton (*ICC*, p. 192) and is taken up by C. A. Moore (*AB*, p. 30).
[3] So K. V. H. Ringgren (*ATD* XVI, p. 385), referred to by C. A. Moore (*AB*, p. 30) and judged by him to be 'not without merit'.
[4] Robert Gordis, 'Studies in the Esther Narrative', *JBL* 95.1 (1976), pp. 47f.
[5] *Ibid.*, p. 48.

(22), and, though his Jewish identity is known, there is no reason for the inference to be made that Esther is also Jewish. It makes good sense for her to avoid any trouble that might arise out of her nationality by keeping quiet on the subject.[1]

Had it not been necessary to keep her identity to herself Esther would surely have secured for Mordecai a position within the palace. As it was she rewarded him for his kindness in bringing her up as his daughter, but without jeopardizing her own safety. Nevertheless, the promotion of Mordecai to the king's gate was sufficient to provoke Haman to anger (5:13).

Meanwhile from his vantage-point Mordecai played the detective and ferreted out the plot on the king's life. As guardians of the threshold, *Bigthan*, who may be the Bigtha of 1:10, and *Teresh* guarded with their life the door of the royal apartment, but in doing so they had unique opportunities to conspire against the king. Many monarchs have died at the hands of their own servants, including eventually Ahasuerus. By making known to Esther what was afoot, Mordecai saved the life of the king, who, like the butler in Genesis 40:23, promptly forgot the man who befriended him. The culprits were duly hanged and the incident was recorded in the Court Chronicles of Persia, but Mordecai was not even thanked for his trouble.

## IV. HAMAN TAKES VENGEANCE ON THE JEWS (3:1–15)

### a. Haman's promotion (3:1–6)

Once again King Ahasuerus is shown in an unfavourable light; he is the dupe of his newly appointed prime minister in passing legislation on the implications of which he is inadequately informed.

**1**. *After these things*, that is, after Esther became queen in the seventh year of the reign (2:16) and before the twelfth year (3:7), Haman was exalted to a position second only to the king (*cf.* 10:3). *Hammedatha* does not feature in any known genealogy; most likely it was the name of an immediate ancestor. The *Agagite* is reminiscent of 1 Samuel 15, where Saul is

---

[1] If the king was required to take a wife from one of seven noble families of Persia, as Herodotus asserts (*The Histories* iii. 84), there was every good reason for silence on the subject of descent.

reprimanded for sparing King Agag, leader of the Amalekites against whom he was fighting. There had been enmity between Israel and Amalek since Amalek attacked at Rephidim (Ex. 17:8–16; *cf.* Dt. 25:17–19; 1 Ch. 4:43), before the Israelites reached Sinai. But if Mordecai was of the family of Saul, who failed to fight Agag to the death, by contrast in the recapitulation of the battle Mordecai would not fail or weaken. LXX translates Agagite as 'bully', so adapting the text freely for Greek readers. (*Cf.* 9:24, where LXX for Agagite has 'Macedonian'.)

There is another dimension to Haman's link with Amalek, who 'did not fear God' (Dt. 25:18). 'Amalek's was an act of defiance, predicated on the denial of God's existence, the assumption that chance alone dominates the universe . . . and so [was] that of Haman, a thousand years later.'[1] Mordecai shares certain 'coincidental' similarities with Saul in that his forefather is called Kish and confronts the Agagite as Saul did.

Though Haman may have been ambitious enough to angle for high office, there is a remarkable absence of racial prejudice in this appointment. Although the king owed his life to Mordecai, promotion went to Haman.

**2–3**. To judge by the gate at Persepolis, which was approached by a spacious stairway and was guarded by huge lion-like figures, and which measured sixty by thirty metres, there was room for *all the king's servants* and others besides in the shady recesses of the gate at Susa's palace. Those officially appointed by the king to his service had to stay within the gate of the royal palace.[2] It is still part of eastern courtesy to bow in recognition of age and honour, and there is evidence that Israelite culture was no exception. While obeisance was given supremely to God and the king, suppliants bowed when seeking favour (so Jacob to Esau, Gn. 33:3) or when expressing indebtedness (*e.g.* David to Jonathan, 1 Sa. 20:41). Mordecai stubbornly refused to submit for any reason to Haman; indeed there seems to have been a general lack of respect for this man, otherwise there should have been no need for a royal command that people should bow down to him. Others might conform but Mordecai was no 'yes man'. While the fact that

[1]Abraham D. Cohen, '*Hu Ha-goral*: The Religious Significance of Esther', *Judaism* 23 (1974), p. 124.
[2]Herodotus, *The Histories* iii. 120, speaks of two provincial governors 'sitting near the palace entrance'. *Cf.* Xenophon, *Cyropaedia* viii. 1.6.

he was a Jew (4) would not preclude his bowing down, the faith of the exiles tended to encourage an independence of judgment and action which embarrassed their captors (Dn. 3; 6).

**4.** Mordecai's persistent obstinacy was calculated to provoke a reaction. Those who conformed with reluctance wanted to discover whether any exceptions had been made.

**5-6.** Until the question was put Haman had not noticed Mordecai, but he reacted with furious resolve, and could tolerate no insubordination. Though *filled with fury* Haman calculated that he could wreak vengeance not only on Mordecai but also on all his race, who could turn out to be equally stubborn in their opposition to him. The narrator plays on the similarity of sound between Haman and *hēmâ*, 'wrath'.

## b. The casting of lots (3:7-11)

The author now comes to the subject which, according to many authorities, constitutes the main theme of the book, namely the origin of the feast of Purim (lots).

**7.** *They cast Pur, that is the lot.* The casting of lots was a common practice throughout the ancient East and in certain specified situations it was employed by Israel as a means of guidance (*e.g.* in the allocation of Canaan to the tribes, Jos. 15:1 ff.). By legitimate use of the lot the Lord would make his will known (Pr. 16:33). Haman was also seeking guidance, but in his mind the important thing was to choose the lucky day, favoured by the omens, for his enterprise, even though it meant waiting a whole year before he could act. *Nisan* and *Adar* occur also in Nehemiah 2:1 and Ezra 6:15; the Hebrew names for the months gave place to the Persian names after the exile.

**8-9.** Haman is careful to ingratiate himself with the king by appearing to be motivated only by *the king's profit*. The king was discouraged from verifying the facts by Haman's omission of all specific details, especially the name of the trouble-makers. That they are *scattered abroad and dispersed* implies that they have retained their identity, and Haman's accusation that they have their own legal system and ignore the laws of the Persian kingdom brands them as guilty. Thus Haman paves the way for the suggestion that they should be destroyed, while in the same breath he promises financial benefit into the bargain. Now for the first time we learn that Haman is a man of wealth; the sum he promises is a vast fortune, and while it is probable that he was planning to take over the property of the Jewish families he annihilated, his proposition would have been ludicrous if he had not had money already at his disposal.

Haman's presentation of his plan is a subtle mixture of truth, half-truth and lies, in that order. While it was true that the Jews had their own laws, it was false to accuse them of disobeying the law of the state.

The word translated *treasuries* is another Persian word. The author was familiar with the vocabulary of the court at Susa. The planned massacre, gruesome though it was, was not without precedents. In 522 BC, at the time of King Cambyses' death, Smerdis the Magus usurped the throne. When he was put to death in a conspiracy every Persian in the capital took up his weapons and killed every Magus he could find.[1] If darkness had not put an end to the slaughter, the whole caste would have been exterminated.

**10.** The king, presuming that the scattered people in question were distant aliens, hostile to his cause, handed over his royal authority to Haman. His *signet ring* was the seal of executive power, recognized throughout the empire. Haman had a free hand to put into effect his far-reaching plot. The author ominously repeats his full title, but adds *the enemy of the Jews*.

**11.** *The money is given to you.* The king may appear to be refusing the money, but it is more likely that he is still expecting Haman to pay it to him, so carrying out the plan as it seemed *good* to him. Words like 'good' take on an alien meaning in the mouth of a tyrant, but the author withholds comment. He has presented a situation in which it is possible to trace some of the varied motives which may interact when national policies are decided. On this occasion the powerful motive of personal revenge was hidden from the king.

The modern reader is fascinated by psychological motivation, and the question why anyone should wish to annihilate the Jews is an important one which still faces the historian,

---

[1] Herodotus, *The Histories* iii. 64–80. 'The anniversary of this day has become a red-letter day in the Persian calendar, marked by an important festival known as the Magophonia, or Killing of the Magi, during which no Magus is allowed to show himself – every member of the caste stays indoors till the day is over' (79).

because attempts to do so continue to the present day. It is, however, doubtful whether the author was as concerned with human psychology as with the divine purpose behind the events he records. Though he maintains a strictly factual and objective stance, the question of ultimate power is never far from the surface. And how powerful is the great King Artaxerxes? Already the writer has shown him let down in public by his wife and taken in by his minister. Will he indeed have control in his home and empire?

### c. The edict sent out (3:12–15)

The drawing up of the edict, its translation into all the languages of the empire and the writing of the final despatches is described in some detail.

**12.** The date, possibly part of the contents of the official wording, was memorable to any Jew because it was the day before the slaying of the Passover lamb (Ex. 12:6). That memorial celebration, with its rehearsal of God's deliverance from the Pharaoh, could scarcely fail to provoke the question, can our God not save us in an equally decisive way from death under Ahasuerus? Because faith believed the answer to be in the affirmative, the liturgy year after year was relevant (Ex. 12:24–27), but it faced a decisive test.

*Satraps*, an adaptation of a Persian word, were the rulers of the twenty satrapies, the *governors* were in charge of the provinces, and the *princes*, better 'officials', were locally promoted (*cf.* comment on 1:3). Though Haman drew up the edict, it went out under the king's seal and in his name. The uniquely engraved seal served as the king's signature.

**13.** The 'royal mail' carried the king's despatches by express couriers on horseback to the farthest bounds of the empire (*cf.* comment on 8:10). *Destroy, slay, annihilate*: the threefold expression is a stylistic feature of legal documents and reflects 'the age-old predilection of officialdom for legalistic terminology that has survived through the ages, in present-day America [and we could add Britain] no less than in ancient Persia'.[1] The same is true of what follows, though *all Jews, young and old*, being masculine in form, might have been thought to exclude women and children. In this death-warrant

---

[1]Robert Gordis, 'Religion, Wisdom and History in the Book of Esther – A New Solution to an Ancient Crux'. *JBL* 100. 3 (1981), p. 377.

they were specifically included. Eleven months still had to elapse before *the thirteenth of Adar*, Haman's day chosen by lot for the massacre. The plundering of Jewish goods was permitted to provide incentive, but it is still hard to envisage the slaughter taking place by order, from cold.

**14–15**. The decree was to be proclaimed so that suitable preparations could be made. A copy (*patšegen*) is a Persian word which occurs in the Bible only in Ezra and Esther, where it is used six times in its Aramaic and Hebrew forms.

There is skilful use of contrast in the last sentence of the chapter. While the collaborators celebrate, the city of Susa is aghast. The author is sensitive to popular reactions and notes that the ordinary citizen asked himself what lay behind such a drastic decree.

## V. ESTHER AGREES TO INTERCEDE (4:1–17)

### a. Mordecai's passionate outburst (4:1–3)

The picture of cold-blooded Haman, biding his time till he has his propitious date, is in marked contrast with Mordecai's immediate demonstration of mourning. We in the West are so conditioned to keeping our grief private and sometimes, to our peril, unexpressed, that we may pass off Mordecai's demonstrative and noisy lamentation as a mere melodramatic show. Lest we should be so out of tune with the culture of the author (for whom the outward signs of grief were deadly serious), it is necessary for us to put ourselves in the place of Mordecai, who by his pig-headed pride or loyalty to principle brought disaster not merely on himself but on his whole race. The punishment is grossly out of proportion to the crime, and suggests that something akin to anti-Semitism was already present in embryo among the populations of the lands of the Dispersion.

**1**. Mordecai, always in the know, lost no time in discovering what lay behind the decree that had just been published (7). Then he *rent his clothes and put on sackcloth and ashes*. These customs are referred to at widely separated periods in the Old Testament (*e.g.* Gn. 37:34; 2 Sa. 1:11; Is. 3:24; Dn. 9:3) and are practised by other nations (Is. 15:3; Ezk. 27:30–33) as well as by Israel. Indeed the Persians of Xerxes' time in Susa are recorded as having torn their clothes in unappeasable grief after their defeat at Salamis.[1] Mordecai was therefore behaving in a way which was in keeping with local practice as well as with Jewish custom in tearing his garments.

**2**. The law against the wearing of sackcloth in the king's gate is not otherwise attested, but it is intrinsically credible (*cf.* Ne. 2:2). Evidently the wearing of sackcloth was known also in Persia, but why should the king be reminded of disasters by having mourners within his gates?

**3**. In every place the Jews reacted as Mordecai had done on hearing the decree. Communal mourning, with fasting, weeping, lamenting and the wearing of sackcloth and ashes, was no formality, but expressed grief and terror such as would prompt repentance and prayer before God, though the writer mentions neither.[2] The prayer of Lamentations 3:40–66 could have been written for the occasion (*cf.* Ezr. 8:21, 23; Ne. 9:1). The spontaneous spreading of sackcloth and ashes so that Jews could prostrate themselves in grief (*cf.* Is. 58:5) is a moving example of national mourning, similar to that of Nineveh (Jon. 3:5–9), but rarely reported even in the Bible.

## b. Esther takes the lead (4:4–17)

Communication between the queen and Mordecai had to be through mediators, even when so secret a matter as is here recorded was under discussion. The utter trustworthiness of Hathach, the royal eunuch, is impressive, and contrasts with the treachery of Bigthan and Teresh (2:21).

**4**. Those who waited on Esther knew of the bond between her and Mordecai, but were not to know that they were related, and the decree which was the talk of the city was evidently as yet unknown in the palace (6–8). When news reached Esther that Mordecai was in mourning she assumed that some material loss had occurred, and so sent him new clothes to wear; but his grief was not to be so easily appeased. Those commentators may be right who argue that Esther's intention in sending clothing to Mordecai was that he should qualify to enter the palace, but in that case his refusal to accept them was extremely discourteous. It would nevertheless be in keeping with his awkwardness which caused the crisis in the first place.

[1]Herodotus, *The Histories* viii. 99.
[2]Possible reasons for his reticence are discussed in the Introduction, p. 35.

**5**. The name *Hathach* may be derived from Persian *hātaka*, 'good'; if so, this man lived up to his name. Ahasuerus had been careful to choose for his queen a man of integrity to wait on her, and had been willing to release him from his own company of retainers.

**6**. There is nothing private about the meeting between Hathach and Mordecai, which took place in the market square, beyond the palace gate, where everyone congregated.

**7–8**. Mordecai did not hesitate to disclose all the exact information, with special attention to the financial inducement that Haman had offered to the king. Rich though he undoubtedly was, Ahasuerus still responded to promise of even greater wealth, though he had repudiated it (3:11). The betrayal of people in exchange for money has always been particularly repugnant (never more so than when Judas betrayed Jesus), and Esther could be counted on to react with passionate resentment. A copy of the decree would silence any doubts about the accuracy of the information, and raise the question, What should be done? Was the decree 'posted' on the city wall for all to see and read?

Mordecai's last word ordered her to use her influence with the king on behalf of her people. He still told her what to do even though she was queen! Touches such as this which are true to life give the story great human appeal.

**9–10**. Hathach the messenger has one responsibility, namely to report with accuracy the message he is given. Direct speech now conveys the conversation.

**11**. Access to the king was strictly controlled, as everyone knew. Like every head of state Ahasuerus needed to be protected both from attempts on his life and from vexation with people's problems. Not that he sat days at a time in isolated splendour on his secluded throne. He gave audiences, at his own discretion and by his personal invitation, but even his wife had no right of approach.[1] Like everyone else she

---

[1]A. T. Olmstead describes the innermost courts of the palace of Susa. 'North of the most private court is the harem, where we may imagine the haughty ladies of the imperial court . . . After traversing various small vestibules, we find three entrances leading down into the private courtyard, for the entire harem is raised 10 inches (perhaps by later restoration).

'To the northwest of the palace complex was located the throne room . . . . The great throne room was 192¾ feet square, its roof supported by six rows of six mighty columns each. To the east and west, the throne room was approached by porticoes of two rows of six more of these columns to a depth of 57⅓ feet. To north and west, below the level of the platform, traces of

appeared between the columns of the throne room at her peril. 'This is most improbable', says Paton, who is judging the situation by modern western society, though he refers to Herodotus who records that after the building of the royal palace at Ecbatana, 'Deioces introduced for the first time the ceremonial of royalty: admission to the king's presence was forbidden, and all communications had to be through messengers. Nobody was allowed to see the king.'[1] Though later practice may have been read back into tradition, the evidence is still valid for later times, and Herodotus shows it in operation at the time of the accession of Darius Hystaspes, who overthrew two usurpers within the palace.[2] Sentries undoubtedly took messages to the king from the gate, so making appointments for an audience. Esther for some reason did not attempt to request an audience. Other people often have easier access to her husband than a wife, who has sometimes to reckon with volatile feelings and reactions, in so sensitive a relationship. Polygamy must have compounded the difficulties. Nevertheless the law had been passed with lawless intruders and not lawful wives in mind. That Esther had not been called to the king *these thirty days* is just one more indication how abnormal life was in the palace at Susa.

**12–14.** *They told. . .* Hathach no longer acts as sole messenger. The answer of Mordecai presents the inmost convictions of the author and at the same time moves the reader to deep sympathy with Esther. Her dilemma is at some time the dilemma of us all: circumstances hem us in and demand that we commit ourselves to act courageously and exercise faith. There are three lines to Mordecai's argument. *i.* Esther herself will not be exempt from destruction under the edict, so in any event her life is in danger. *ii.* Mordecai reveals his own conviction that God will not permit the extinction of his people. If Esther fails, God will have another way of saving the Jews, but Esther and her immediate family will be the losers. There is here an incidental reference to one aspect of guidance. God's purposes are not thwarted by the

---

kiosks indicate the position of the paradise or garden, easily watered from the near-by river and protected by a tower at the northwestern corner' (*HPE*, p. 170). Though Persepolis was administratively less important than Susa its buildings have been better preserved. *Cf.* E. F. Schmidt, *Persepolis* I, II, III, (Chicago, 1953, 1957, 1968). See also articles by M. Roth in *Iran* 21.

[1]*The Histories* i. 99. Tradition made him founder of the Median empire.
[2]*The Histories* iii. 77, 84, 118, 140.

failure of one individual to respond positively to his leading, and the individual is truly free to refuse it, though this leads to loss rather than gain. *iii.* The right way forward is not in doubt. The outcome of Esther's decision is so far-reaching that without exaggeration she is at the moment when her life's purpose is at stake.

*And who knows whether you have not come to the kingdom for such a time as this?* Without explicitly spelling out in detail how he came to his convictions, Mordecai reveals that he believes in God, in God's guidance of individual lives, and in God's ordering of the world's political events, irrespective of whether those who seem to have the power acknowledge him or not. This was, of course, constantly declared by the prophets of Israel (*e.g.* Is. 10:8 ff.; 45:1; Je. 1:15; Ezk. 7:24), and need not come as a surprise, especially in the light of the return from exile in 538 and subsequent occasions (Ezr. 1–2; 5–6). Every Jew had experienced in the history of his people the guiding and saving hand of God. Many of our contemporaries recognized that same overruling during the crises of the Second World War.

**15–16**. Esther's reply is also a confession of faith, though it is not couched in overtly religious language. She implies that she accepts the suggestion of Mordecai as her duty, but that she is full of apprehension at the thought of fulfilling it. By asking that all the Jews in Susa join her in a fast Esther acknowledges that *i.* she needs the support and fellowship of others and *ii.* she depends on more than human courage Though prayer is not mentioned, it was always the accompaniment of fasting in the Old Testament, and the whole point of fasting was to render the prayer experience more effective and prepare oneself for communion with God (Ex. 34:28; Dt. 9:9; Jdg. 20:26; Ezr. 8:21–23). 'In practice, fasting in the setting of religious rites and as a defence against trouble was common in the whole of the ancient world.'[1] Persians would therefore have thought it strange if the Jews had not called a fast at such a time. For Esther, Isaac Watts' hymn would have been appropriate, had it been written in her day:

> I'm not ashamed to own my Lord
> Or to defend His cause.

[1] F. S. Rothenberg, *DNTT* I, p. 612, 'Fast'.

The poet implies an admission that the possibility of failure at a time of testing has to be reckoned with. The words are therefore in the nature of a prayer for boldness such as Esther is sure to have prayed during her days of fasting.

*Neither eat nor drink for three days.* Fasting was usually for one day only. It was obligatory on the Day of Atonement (Lv. 16:29–31), but otherwise fasting was undertaken as a voluntary act for a particular occasion (1 Sa. 14:24; 2 Sa. 1:12). Esther's three-day fast indicated the seriousness with which she regarded the emergency and her own need of strength. Feasting, and in particular drinking, play a prominent part in this book; here the word 'drink' is used in the context of a fast. 'The auxiliary motif of fasting contrasts and highlights the motif of feasting in Esther.'[1] *Night or day* is a reminder that, as in the Islamic fast of Ramadan meals are permitted during the night, the fast could have been confined to certain hours.

*Then I will go to the king, though it is against the law* (lit. 'not according to the decree'). These words sum up the problems of conscience that face believers in many situations today, and divide the church. If it were not for the fact that people like Martin Luther King and countless others have lost their lives in opposing powerful majorities, we might think that Esther's *if I perish, I perish* was over-dramatic. Certainly Jesus promised that words to say would be given to his followers when they were brought to trial, but not that they would be acquitted (Mk. 13:11–12).

**17.** From this point on Esther, who had up till now done as Mordecai told her, herself takes the lead and assumes responsibility in her own right.

## Additional Note: Fasting

The practice of fasting in the book of Esther contrasts with the more dominant note of feasting. The most usual Hebrew verb, *ṣûm*, occurs four times in the book: 4:3; 4:16 (twice); 9:31. First there is the spontaneous reaction of the Jews throughout the Persian empire to bewail the king's decree (4:3). The mourning, fasting, weeping, lamenting and wearing of sackcloth and ashes were genuine expressions of dismay at the impending disaster, but that is all. Esther's fast (4:16) was

[1]Berg, p. 37.

similarly an expression of distress over the anticipated death and destruction of the Jews, but it had an added significance. By seeking a way out of the dilemma Esther raised the hope of a future for the community after all. In 9:31 the reference is to commemorative fasts which, while contrasting with the joyous festival, were in keeping with the fasting that was an integral part of the original event.

To judge by the frequent mention of fasting in the post-exilic books of the Old Testament, a new earnestness characterized God's people after the destruction of Jerusalem. Abstinence from food and drink on occasions for special reasons was undoubtedly practised in pre-exilic Israel (Ex. 34:28; 1 Sa. 28:20; 2 Sa. 12:16–17; 1 Ki. 21:27–29), and the annual fast on the Day of Atonement was built into Israel's liturgical calendar (Lv. 16:29–34). But from the time of the exile onwards the subject is mentioned relatively frequently, as though the shock of Jerusalem's destruction had added a degree of seriousness to the way in which communion with God was regarded, and well it might. The personification of Jerusalem in the laments expresses something of the bereavement felt by her population:

> How lonely sits the city
> that was full of people!
> How like a widow has she become,
> she that was great among the nations!
> She that was a princess among the cities
> has become a vassal.
> She weeps bitterly in the night,
> tears on her cheeks;
> among all her lovers
> she has none to comfort her;
> all her friends have dealt treacherously with her,
> they have become her enemies (La. 1:1–2).

If only the warnings had been heeded destruction could have been averted (Je. 7:1–7), but the example of Samaria's fate failed to strike Jerusalem's leaders as of any relevance (Ezk. 16:46–52), and the gracious deliverance of the capital when Assyria had almost been victorious (2 Ki. 18:17 – 19:37) was turned into a guarantee of eternal immunity. Jeremiah had to bear the brunt of popular ridicule and public contradiction when he used every means he could devise to give warning of the pending tragedy (*e.g.* Je. 19 – 20).

When the war was over disillusionment was extreme, vitality was sapped (Ezk. 33:10), and Ezekiel found himself dealing with perverse ideas of God's alleged injustice (Ezk. 33:17,24). Fast days to commemorate the stages of Jerusalem's fall probably met a communal need to come to terms with shock and guilt (Zc. 7:2–3; *cf.* 8:19). In a liturgical prayer for such a fast day Daniel poured out the confession of his people's sins and claimed on the ground of God's great mercy the forgiveness which alone could prepare the way for restoration (Dn. 9). The prayers and visions of Daniel put him under such strain that for him fasting was as much the dictate of his body as of his spirit (Dn. 8:27; 9:3; 10:2–3). The prayer of chapter 9 is priestly in character, despite the fact that Daniel was not from the priestly tribe; Ezra, on the other hand, was of the line of Aaron (Ezr. 7:5). He called for a fast before he started out for Jerusalem with returning exiles of his generation, to whom had been entrusted Temple treasures to be handed over safely on arrival (Ezr. 8). Nehemiah, like Esther, had to find favour with the king (in his case Artaxerxes I) if he was to fulfil the organizational role to which he believed that the Lord was calling him. He therefore prayed with fasting until the opportunity arose for him to put his case before the king (Ne. 1:4 – 2:8). A day of communal fasting is recorded in connection with the renewal of the covenant (Ne. 9:1ff.). Positive signs of answered prayer are recorded in situations where specific requests are made.

Nevertheless not all occasions of fasting produced the desired results. In Isaiah 58:3 the question is raised why this should be, and a definitive answer is given. Fasting in and of itself was of no interest to the Lord unless it was accompanied by just dealing and righteous ways. Ascetic practices were morally neutral, not meritorious. Yet the idea of gaining merit by fasting persisted and hardened into an element of piety, which together with almsgiving and prayer drew the commentary of Jesus in the sermon on the mount (Mt. 6:1–18). There is no trace of such an attitude to fasting in the book of Esther, but in setting up legislation for any religious observance there is always the possibility that formalism will obscure its original intention. That, however, is the lesser evil; it would be worse if the gracious intervention of God it called to mind were to be entirely forgotten.

Two further questions arise: *i.* What of fasting in the life of the Christian? *ii*. Is feasting more appropriate? Though Jesus fasted before beginning his ministry and assumed that the Twelve would fast (Mt. 6:16), he did not expect them to fast while he was with them (Mt. 9:15). The bridegroom was indeed taken away from them, and for a short time they fasted, but the resurrection ushered in the new era of rejoicing and they would never again be desolate (Jn. 14:18). The fast days of the Jewish calendar did not continue in the Christian liturgy, and the subject of fasting is scarcely mentioned outside the Synoptic Gospels in the New Testament.[1] The gospel of salvation by grace alone ruled out altogether any meritorious contribution on the part of the penitent sinner, whose faith in Jesus Christ for salvation was demonstrated in baptism (Acts 2:38–39), and great was the joy generated by the gift of the Holy Spirit among the believers (Acts 2:46–47). They were indeed nearer to feasting than to fasting, but not to the selfishness and over-indulgence that characterized Persian and other feasts. The church at Corinth had to be rebuked for its failure to eat and drink worthily at the Lord's supper (1 Cor. 11:20–22, 27–32), but despite the solemnity of that meal the dominant note was overwhelming joy in Christ.

Is there, then, any place at all for fasting in the Christian life? Not as a way of gaining merit, nor as a religious exercise used to impress others, and certainly not as a means of 'twisting God's arm'. But, just as the church at Antioch fasted and prayed when Paul and Barnabas were commissioned, and the mainly gentile churches of Asia Minor prayed and fasted over the appointment of their elders (Acts 13:3; 14:23), so fasting may have its place in the church today. *i*. In an age of rush one way of making time for prayer is to forgo a meal. *ii*. Life's inequalities offer opportunities to help provide for others by taking less of the world's resources for ourselves. *iii*. Prayer with fasting ensures that important decisions that come in one's personal life and in the church are being taken with due seriousness. *iv*. When a whole community prays and fasts together, as in the Esther crisis, all share in the joy of seeing God's response and give praise to him (*cf.* 2 Cor. 1:11). Even unborn generations enter into the thanksgiving. It is rarely that the church as a whole is called to pray with fasting.

[1]The Greek word *nēsteia* occurs twice in Paul's letters (2 Cor. 6:5; 11:27), but each time the context suggests that the meaning is enforced hunger rather than deliberate fasting. In Acts 13:3 and 14:23, however, the word is being used in a religious sense.

Perhaps, living as we do under the shadow of the nuclear threat, the enormity of the crisis numbs even the will to seek God's mercy, but resignation is not among the Christian virtues. The example of Esther may serve to remind the Christian church of the place that fasting has in seeking God's face at a time of crisis.

## VI. ESTHER FINDS FAVOUR (5:1-14)

### a. Esther's petition (5:1-8)

**1.** *On the third day* of the fast Esther knew she had to act on her resolve without further delay, and appear before the king. *Her royal robes* (Heb. *malkût*, 'royalty') demonstrated that she approached the king as one with privileged status as the king's consort. She presented herself, albeit with due deference, as the king's counterpart (*cf.* Gn. 2:18, 'a helper fit for him'), her beauty enhanced by the queenly robes. No doubt these were in keeping with the king's splendid robes of Phoenician purple, heavy with gold embroidery, worn over garments of white and purple, but suitably subdued by comparison to avoid detracting from the glory of the 'lord of all the earth', before whom all who entered had to prostrate themselves.[1] The exact meaning of the words translated *king's palace* and *king's hall* is not altogether certain, mainly because it has not been possible to identify the ruined structures at Susa to the extent that the palace of Persepolis has been identified and reconstructed. There the *apadana* or 'hall of pillars', modelled on that at Susa, with its thirty-six columns, soared up to a height of 65 feet. Its pillars were 'the most slender and airy columns ever produced by the hand of man'.[2] This was the throne room into which Esther dared to step and stand within the view of the king, contrary to the law.

**2.** The columns were not permitted to obscure the vision of the king as he sat upon his throne, and when he caught sight of Queen Esther in all her regal beauty and realized that only some weighty problem would have induced her to appear

---

[1]*HPE*, pp. 282f. 'By ancient oriental custom the king is in a very real sense a divinity', comments Olmstead.

[2]*HPE*, p. 281. Incidentally the tiers of apartments which housed the royal harem were in complete contrast. 'Each tier consisted of a tiny hall whose roof was upheld by only four columns, and a bedroom so minute that even with a single occupant the atmosphere must have been stifling' (*ibid.*, p. 285).

before him unbidden, he extended to her the golden sceptre. The king's movement of his sceptre indicates that Esther is to approach and touch the tip of it, to symbolize her acceptance.[1] The dramatic tension between human relationships and the overriding demands of royal protocol is always full of fascination.

**3.** *What is it* (lit. 'what to you'), *Queen Esther?* The terse Hebrew idiom may shed some light on the ever-difficult question of Jesus to his mother, 'what have you to do with me?' (Jn. 2:4). Commentators usually remark on the extravagance of the king's vow to grant anything to Esther, *even to the half of my kingdom.* The repetition of the expression (v. 6) suggests that it was a conventional phrase (*cf.* its very different setting in Mk. 6:23). The declaration of the marriage service, 'with all my worldy goods I thee endow', and its modern wording, 'all that I have I share with you', is in any case far more extravagant in its generosity.

**4.** Esther's request is an anti-climax, which nevertheless is in keeping with protocol, for a formal state occasion is no place for the queen to disclose her mind. Though they are not mentioned, retainers would be present, as well as guards and other officials.[2] The dinner-party, though not without its attendants, would be much less public and formal, and the king would assume that the question of the request was his to raise again. It was a daring move to invite Haman to the dinner as the only guest of the royal couple, and yet it would be perfectly in keeping with the king's recent promotion of this man (3:1), whom he had made his equal and friend (3:10, 15), and would therefore occasion no surprise. The days of corporate fasting, accompanied by prayer, had given to Esther a wisdom from above, and a confidence not her own. She had even prepared the meal, believing that the outcome of her daring initiative would be favourable.

**5.** His last audience of the day over, the king, aware more of his hunger than of his supposed divinity, is not slow to *do*

[1]See *IBD* I, p. 363 for a photograph of the relief from Persepolis, showing the Persian king Darius I holding his sceptre in his right hand and a lotus in his left. *Cf.* Peter Calmeyer on this verse in *Archäologische Mitteilungen aus Iran* 13 (Berlin, 1980), pp. 59–61.

[2]Two personal attendants accompanied the king. Olmstead describes them thus: 'One holds over his master's head the royal parasol ... which must accompany the king even on a military expedition; the other, the chamberlain, bears napkin and fly-flapper' (*HPE*, p. 283). *Cf.* M. Roaf, 'Sculptures and Sculptors at Persepolis' in *Iran* 21, and E. F. Schmidt, *Persepolis* III.

*as Esther desires.* Omission of her title is a homely touch in contrast to verse 3. Did they relax sufficiently to remove their crowns? It seems that the king still carried his sceptre on such an occasion (8:4).

**6.** Once the leisurely eastern feast was over, the three reclined on their couches (*cf.* 1:6) and drank wine, an occupation that our writer takes every opportunity to point out. *Your petition . . . your request.* The balancing of conventional words and cadences captures the slow rhythm of the east.

**7-8.** Esther answers in similarly stately phraseology (*cf.* 8:5). There is no hurry about the request she wishes to make. Let there be another such enjoyable meal together, and then she will disclose her petition.[1]

### b. Haman's vexation (5:9-14)

Esther the hostess has been directing developments during her dinner-party, but now the narrator allows us to see what happens to each of the guests immediately afterwards.

**9.** Haman was on top of the world at the unexpected honour that had come his way, and left the palace in convivial good humour, but he got no further than the king's gate before his joy was checked. Mordecai, his fast ended, had discarded his sackcloth and was back in his usual seat to taunt Haman by his studied indifference to Haman's pre-eminence. In keeping with his calculating temperament, Haman does not immediately allow his wrath full rein, but bides his time.

**10.** Back in his house everyone has to hear Haman's impressions of the party. His *friends* turn out to be his council of advisers (6:13), experts in court matters; but his wife is an active adviser too. The name *Zeresh,* like most of the names in the book, is of uncertain spelling and meaning.[2]

**11.** As 'fools proclaim their folly' (Pr. 12:23), so Haman

---

[1]In general, the king breakfasted and dined alone, though on occasion he might be joined by the queen or by his sons' (*HPE,* p. 183).

[2]The six versions of the text tabled by C. A. Moore (*AB,* p. xlii) have five different spellings from *zōsaran* (lxx) to *zares* (Vulgate); English versions follow the MT. Paton (*ICC,* p. 89) gives details of Jensen's attempt to link the name with Girisha or Kirisha, an Elamite goddess and consort of Humman, so attempting to indicate a mythical basis to the story. Later Jensen himself rejected this derivation in favour of one from Siris, Babylonian goddess of wine, but neither derivation has established itself. H. S. Gehman (*JBL* 43 (1924), p. 327) suggests 'one with dishevelled hair'. Fortunately the meaning of the name is not important for an understanding of the story.

could not conceal the extent of his prosperity. His order of priorities puts his riches in first place, even before his sons, who we learn later were ten in number (9:7–10), but uppermost in his thoughts are the recent honours which give him precedence over every other subject in the kingdom.

**12**. Haman is so sure that his advancement makes good sense that he does not suspect that Esther may have any ulterior motive in issuing a second invitation to dine with the monarch and herself.

**13**. All this *does me no good* (Heb. *šoweh*); the translation of this word is flexible. In 3:8 the meaning is 'not suitable for' [the king]; in 7:4 RSV translates 'not to be compared with'; the idea in our verse is that all his gains are outweighed by the one killjoy, Mordecai. Despite the fact that Haman had already laid his plans for ridding himself of this man, in his present mood Haman's irritation is becoming beyond endurance.

**14**. The initiative in suggesting a course of action comes from his wife, supported by the 'friends'. *A gallows* (Heb. *ʿēṣ*) is literally 'tree'; it could have been a pole or indeed anything made of wood. The word haunts the book (*cf.* 2:23; 6:4; 7:9–10; 8:7; 9:13, 25). The height of the gallows, 75 feet, strikes western commentators as exaggerated. It certainly is unnecessarily high, but then everything constructed by Persian rulers was on a grand scale, like the image of Babylonian Nebuchadrezzar (Dn. 3:1), which was 10 cubits (15 feet) higher. *Then go merrily . . . to the dinner.* The connection between murder and merriment and Haman's pleasure is even more sinister than the gallows he had made.

## VII. HAMAN INADVERTENTLY PROMOTES MORDECAI (6:1–13)

This is a chapter of coincidences and yet there is no detail of it which in itself is unbelievable. No-one acts in a way that is out of character; indeed it is the very predictability of Haman's self-glorification that makes for such intense dramatic irony when Haman has to eat the dust and honour his hated enemy.

## a. The king's bedtime book (6:1–3)

When many thousands of his poorest subjects were asleep, 'the head that wore a crown' was wide awake and *could not sleep*, lit. 'sleep fled' (*cf.* Gn. 31:40, where RSV keeps the Hebrew idiom). Even these days, with our sleeping-pills, the hypnotic effect of a droning human voice is a recognized way of inducing sleep. But maybe the king had given up all hope of sleep that night and decided to make up arrears in checking the records of his reign. The *book of memorable deeds* (*cf.* Mal. 3:16 for its heavenly counterpart) would be the source from which the king's honours list was drawn up, and as a general rule special services were promptly rewarded.[1] That the king should have failed to honour one who had saved his life was a serious omission that clearly needed to be dealt with, and some specially noteworthy reward devised, if the king's reputation for just dealing was to be maintained.

## b. Haman's humiliation (6:4–13)

One way of arriving at an honour that was sure to be appreciated was to ask the recipient what gift he would like to receive, but on this occasion the king could permit no further delay.

**4.** In the early morning, when even the guards could not be counted upon to be at their posts, the court was empty but for one man. Haman also had been at work all night, seeing to the erection of gallows, and, spurning sleep, had come long before the usual time to the king's court in order to make sure that he had his necessary interview with the king and could carry out Mordecai's execution. Even so important a person as Haman might be frustrated by a long list of appointments, and at least he would be first in the queue.

**5.** His immediate summons into the king's presence was an unexpected privilege that augured well from his point of view. *Standing* is a literal translation of a verb (Heb. *'āmad*) which is flexible in meaning; in 3:4 it is translated 'avail' and in 7:7 'stayed', a meaning which it could have here: 'Haman is there,

---

[1]Herodotus gives five examples of such rewards, three of them in the reign of Darius (iii. 138, 140; v. 11) and two in Xerxes' reign (viii. 85; ix. 107). Xerxes in the former reference invested two men with land, and enrolled one of them 'in the catalogue of the king's Benefactors' (Persian *orosangae*). In the second passage Xerxes rewarded one who saved the life of his brother with governorship of the whole of Cilicia.

waiting . . . .

**6**. There was a meeting of persons but not of minds. Of course the king expected to hear just what his courtier would himself like to receive by way of honours, and anyone might have made the mistake of Haman in assuming that he was to be promoted. The irony lay in what had been happening during the night both to the king and to Haman, and the conflicting intentions of each.

**7–9**. Haman repeats exactly words the king himself used, *the man whom the king delights to honour*, as though ruminating over them. The suggestion he goes on to make reveals how important prestige was to him. When he could have asked for a governorship or riches, he wanted to dress up in the king's robes, and ride around on the king's horse wearing its crown, and heralded with his citation. He takes an almost childish delight in the idea of receiving public acclaim for what he has already enjoyed in the privacy of the palace, namely near equality with the king. The horse's *crown* can be seen from reliefs on the east stairway of the Apadana at Persepolis to be a special arrangement of the horse's hair to form a topknot between the ears.[1] That Haman wanted to ride the king's horse could have appeared to be a bid for the throne (1 Ki. 1:33), but in the event no such problem arose.

**10–11**. Haman was to be the 'most noble prince' who carried out the investiture of the very person he was about to hang. The king seems to be ignorant of the mutual antagonism between these two; in his isolation he had no means of knowing what was evident to a child playing at the gate of his palace, but citizens who watched the parade through the city square could appreciate the irony and marvel at the incongruity. The words Haman had to proclaim must have been gravel in his mouth. In the eyes of the crowd he was already finished.

**12**. Incongruity continues as Mordecai returns to the king's gate. Whether or not he is still wearing the king's robes, the episode has achieved nothing that makes any difference to the status of Mordecai. He has merely taken part in official play-acting. Haman for his part is utterly humiliated, and admits as much by his public mourning.

**13**. The involvement of Zeresh in her husband's plight suggests that this marriage went deeper than Esther's with the king could ever go, and intensifies the tragedy of what is

[1] See *AB*, Plate 4.

to follow. Now that everything is going wrong for Haman his personal advisers make it sound as if they had nothing to do with the course of action Haman had pursued. *If Mordecai . . . is of the Jewish people* implies that they had not known this detail, whereas Haman had called him Mordecai 'the Jew' (5:13). This is only the first step in isolating Haman, now that he is in trouble. *You have begun to fall . . . you will not prevail . . .* you *will surely fall* before him. Behind this cold comfort there seems to lie commonly accepted folk wisdom, perhaps proverbial. The way in which the Jewish people had survived deportations and preserved their identity had not escaped notice, and this in itself witnessed to the power of their God (*cf.* Ezk. 38:23). The deliverance of the individual, Mordecai, just though it is, needs to be seen as part of this wider purpose of God to bring glory to his own name and to establish his kingdom. That this was no accident could be shown by reference to Edom, a nation of similar size, which did not survive the Babylonian experience even though it was not deported (Mal. 1:2–5). The continuing survival of the Jewish people to the present day is also a continuing witness to the world that the Lord is great, 'beyond the border of Israel'.

## VIII. QUEEN ESTHER'S SECOND FEAST (6:14 – 7:10)

**14**. Events now move swiftly. Haman was still trying to come to terms with the change in his circumstances when eunuchs, sent by the king to escort Haman to the feast in accordance with custom, arrived at his door. They *brought Haman in haste*. It is true that the Hebrew could have the sense of 'hurrying out of eagerness', as in 2:9, and Moore thinks the verb intensified Haman's importance.[1] In the circumstances, however, there could well be a hint here that Haman in his dismay had delayed his preparations, felt himself to be no longer in control of events and therefore at a disadvantage. Even he dared not keep the king waiting.

**7:1–2**. *On the second day*, as on the first (5:6), while relaxing over the wine at the end of the meal, the king repeated his invitation to Esther, but this time using her title *Queen Esther*, as in 5:3. The courtesy was encouraging in so tricky a situation.

[1]*AB*, p. 69. *Cf.* Paton (*ICC*, p. 257), who says, 'the expression *hastened* means no more than *brought expeditiously*'.

**3.** For her part Queen Esther returned the courtesy, using the deferential address appropriate, but omitted by Haman in 6:7, when putting a suggestion before the king. *My life . . . my people.* The terse statement was full of pent-up feeling, and would raise more questions than it answered in the mind of the king, whose curiosity was now fully aroused.

**4.** *For we are sold* is a reference to financial gain offered by Haman as an inducement to the king to grant his request (3:9). The verb was not always used literally (*cf.* Dt. 32:30; Jdg. 2:14; 4:9; Ps. 44:12), but in the light of the money transaction in this case it was doubly appropriate. *To be destroyed, to be slain, and to be annihilated*: the verbs are exactly those of the decree despite the difference required by the English translation (*cf.* 3:13). To emphasize the enormity of the plot it was appropriate to introduce the idea that the queen and her people might have been sold as slaves, as though that would have occasioned no protest. The meaning of the last clause of verse 4 is problematic for several reasons. The word translated *affliction* (Heb. *ṣār*) can also mean 'enemy' (RV 'adversary'), and there is no indication whose affliction is meant. The word for *loss* renders a Hebrew term which occurs only here in the Old Testament, and whose meaning is therefore uncertain, though in rabbinic Hebrew it means 'damage', 'injury'. The translator here also has to be interpreter, hence the wide differences between versions: *e.g.* 'no such distress would justify disturbing the king' (NIV); 'for then our plight would not be such as to injure the king's interests' (NEB); '. . . I would have kept quiet and not bothered you about it' (GNB, a very free translation). The older interpretation appears in the margin of NIV, 'but the compensation our adversary offers cannot be compared with the loss the king would suffer', a sense which JB expresses very well: 'but as things are, it will be beyond the means of the persecutor to make good the loss that the king is about to sustain'. This reference to the king's concerns is good psychology and the inference that people are to be valued above money is in keeping with Esther's cause; so, until more light is shed on the meaning, the last two translations quoted have most to commend them, with RSV a close runner-up.

**5.** In Hebrew the verb *said* occurs twice; this may have originated as a scribal error (dittography), in which case the translator is right to omit one. Perhaps more likely both should be expressed: 'The king interrupted and exlaimed'. Though

Esther has been careful to avoid any reference to Haman, the king wants to know who is responsible for the plot to destroy his queen, and agitatedly asks where the man is who has the audacity (lit. 'fills his heart') to do such a thing.

**6**. *A foe and an enemy!* As Esther has put the case Haman is a traitor to the king as well as an enemy of the Jews. As she points to *this wicked Haman* she senses her triumph and notes the *terror* of Haman. He might well be terrified. Esther's words to the king had been an eye-opener for him also, because he had not known Esther's nationality. The realization that he had inadvertently threatened the queen's life was a knock-out blow on top of his earlier humiliation. She for her part has revealed that she is Jewish, but does not know for sure how the king will receive that information.

**7**. The king's departure enabled Haman the opportunist to make one last bid for an escape from his alarming danger. Having estimated that he stood no chance of mercy from the king, he decided to *beg his life* from one whose life he had threatened, and from a member of the Jewish race which he had scorned. But had she not chosen to request his company, and might she not soften towards him? In the momentary relief of tension caused by the king's departure he would turn his charm on the queen; the irony is evident.

**8**. Etiquette with regard to the harem was so strict that it would have been difficult for Haman to converse with the queen without causing offence. Had he not been so desperate he would no doubt have left with the king, so as to avoid any possible misinterpretation of his remaining behind with the queen. In approaching her as she continued to recline on her couch, as was customary at Persian feasts, Haman was going too far, and by *falling on the couch* he set the seal on his execution. Even had she wished to help there was nothing Esther could have done to save him. The king was outraged. *They covered Haman's face* implies the present of retainers at hand to carry out the king's intentions.[1] Though the practice of covering the heads of condemned prisoners by the Persians in ancient times is otherwise unattested, it was the custom among the Greeks and Romans.

[1]Robert Gordis argues that on grounds of syntax and word order the translation should be, 'And Haman's face was covered'. He thinks an archaic form has caused failure to recognize a participle passive of a *tertiae yodh* verb (*JBL* 95. 1 (1976), p. 56). Even so the active form 'they [indefinite] covered' is a possible translation.

**9**. Once again the king needs to be told what is common knowledge among the palace staff, and Harbona reveals the candid opinion of Haman current among the king's eunuchs, when he draws attention to the gallows prepared for the execution of the man responsible for saving the king's life.

**10**. The king took up the implied suggestion, and there is a certain irony in the exact outworking of justice. Haman was 'hoist with his own petard'.

## IX. AHASUERUS TURNS THE TABLES (8:1–17)

### a. Vacant places filled (8:1–2)

There is evidence that the property of condemned criminals reverted to the crown. This was assumed by the Phoenician Jezebel (1 Ki. 21:7–16) and shown to be operative in Persia in the reign of Darius by Herodotus.[1] The same law operated with regard to Haman's *house*, a word which in Genesis 39:4 is synonymous with 'all that he had'. So here Haman's total estate is meant. This the king bestows on Queen Esther by way of compensation and as a token of good will. Mordecai now comes into his own, for the reward he received through Haman had been both temporary and intangible. His presentation to the king as Esther's close relative and protector became the occasion for his investiture as the king's first minister and executive, in place of Haman. The bestowal of the signet ring conveyed legal authority to act on the king's behalf (*cf.* 3:10). Esther for her part needed an estate manager, a role to which she appointed Mordecai. The fall of Haman had now been totally balanced by the rise of the one he sought to overthrow and destroy.

### b. Reversal of the edict (8:3–14)

**3**. The solidarity of the Jewish people involved loyalty to the thousands whom Haman had destined to destruction, hence Esther's further intercession. Her plea, accompanied this time by prostration and tears, is intended to move the king to mercy. At her second feast it is true that Esther had requested the life of her people, but it became apparent that the king was totally taken up with the threat to the queen's

[1] *The Histories* iii. 128–129. Oroetes the Persian was punished for his betrayal of Polycrates, was killed, and his money confiscated and conveyed to Susa.

life (7:3–5). Now is the moment to achieve the overthrow of Haman's decree and deliver the Jewish people, while opportunity is offered; in view of the fear Haman's decree would have engendered, it is unthinkable that the matter could be delayed.[1] To stop short at that point would have been selfishly to accept personal deliverance without proper concern for the community. In her solidarity with her people and her desire to save them from death Esther shows an understanding of the ideals set by the prophets (esp. Is. 53:12) and sets us an example to follow.

**4–6.** The golden sceptre on this occasion permits Esther to rise, like the dubbed knight in English ceremonial, and stand before the monarch. With due deference she makes her plea. Two of the conventional phrases have already occurred in inverse order in 7:3, but her addition of two other conditions is a measure of the uncertainty she feels in making this further request. *If. . .I be pleasing in his eyes* takes advantage of her current good standing in the eyes of the capricious king. To ask that a law of the Persians be revoked (lit. 'caused to return'; *cf.* Is. 55:11) was virtually to ask the impossible, so Esther avoids the term 'law' and lays stress on the work of Haman. Though strictly the letters had gone out in the name of the king, he had had no knowledge of the plot.

*How can I endure* (lit. 'how am I able to . . .')? The repetition of this verb expresses the depth of Esther's empathy with the sufferings of others. It is very moving to see the extent to which this young girl, who has everything money can buy, identifies herself with her own kith and kin, and is prepared to risk everything in an attempt to prevent the disaster that threatens them.

**7.** There is no reason to question the presence of Mordecai and therefore the inclusion of his name here. *Behold . . .* The kings draws attention to the concessions he has already made to indicate his sympathy with Esther and his good will towards the Jews; *he would lay hands on* is idiomatic for 'conspire against' and should be so translated in Psalm 55:20 and Daniel 11:42 as well as here.[2]

---

[1]Paton, for example, says, 'It is . . . hard to see why Esther should run this risk when the day for slaughtering the Jews was set nearly a year later on (see on 4[11])' (*ICC*, p. 269).

[2]Hayim Tawill has shown that this is the meaning from parallel Akkadian idioms in 'Two Notes on the Treaty Terminology of the Sefire Inscriptions', *CBQ* 42 (1980), pp. 30–37.

**8.** *You may write* (plural). The pronoun 'you', which in Hebrew did not need to be expressed, is not only included but is also in the emphatic first place in the sentence. The effect is to empower Esther and Mordecai together to draft their own decree and send it out under the king's seal. Though it was impossible for the king to take back any word that had gone out in his name, the same effect could be achieved by a later edict, similarly authenticated. He had his ways and means of achieving his will.

**9.** This verse illustrates the author's policy of repeating his previous wording in another context, so creating pairs of situations. Here he recalls the occasion when Haman originated the decree against the Jews, by making this long statement identical with that of 3:12, except for the change of name, date and intention, and a few additions from 1:1. The effect is to draw attention to the suddenness with which an official can rise to power, pass his laws, and just as suddenly fall and be replaced. A comparison of the dates in the two verses, from the thirteenth of the first month to the twenty-third of the third, allows for a longer lapse of time than might have seemed likely (*cf.* such references as 5:1; 6:1, 14; 8:1). *Sivan* (Bab. *Simanu*, third month, May/June) is mentioned only here in the Old Testament. The Babylonian names of the months were adopted in the post-exilic period.

Mordecai took responsibility for drawing up the edict which the king's secretaries had to copy and translate into the many languages of the empire, as in the case of Haman's decree. This time, however, Hebrew was added for the copies sent to the Jews in every province.

**10.** In this reference to the Persian 'royal mail' a few words are somewhat obscure, because they are Hebrew transliterations of Persian technical terms, but the general sense is not in doubt. *Couriers* (Heb. *rāṣîm*) was the word used in 3:13, but this time special comment is made on the *horses* they were permitted to ride. They are referred to by the collective term *rekeš*, which in Micah 1:13 is the word for chariot steeds and in 1 Kings 4:28 (5:8, Heb.) for the 'swift steeds' specially imported by Solomon. These then were the equivalent of today's racehorses, *bred from the royal stud* (lit. 'sons of the royal mares'), though the exact meaning of the last word (Heb. *rammāk*) is dubious. Mordecai evidently went to extreme lengths to ensure the express delivery of his new edict.

**11.** The letters granted to the Jews the king's permission, first, *to gather together* (Heb. *qāhal*), used of assembling for military call-up, political or judicial consultation, and for worship. Can it be that as early as this the right of assembly had been withheld? Secondly, *to defend their lives* and those of their children and wives. A comparison in RSV between this verse and Haman's decree in 3:13, where the order is 'women and children', could suggest that Jewish thinking put wives last. The Hebrew has the same idiom, *ṭap̄ wᵉnāšîm*, in both places, and the order is dictated by nothing more than euphony. The verbs *destroy, slay, annihilate* also keep strictly to the wording of the original decree which Mordecai is reversing; now it is the Jews who will be doing these things. But to whom?

This verse has given rise to the opinion that the Jews sought the right to kill the defenceless women and children of the countries in which they were exiles, and understandably this has raised ethical issues which have caused the book to be condemned. In NEB, JB and GNB the verse is translated in such a way as to eliminate any ambiguity such as is found in RSV and to support the bloodthirsty view that exact revenge was being taken on the total population. GNB, for example, has 'If they were attacked by armed men or any nationality in any province, they could fight back and destroy them along with their wives and children; they could slaughter them to the last man and take their possessions'. Commentators have been almost unanimous that this is the meaning of the text.[1] At the same time they often comment on the improbability that permission would be given by the king for such wholesale slaughter of the Persian population, even though the whole Jewish race had been so threatened. The thought is that this Esther story works out the retribution theme of the Old Testament by permitting, and even glorying in, the outworking of 'an eye for an eye and a tooth for a tooth' (Ex. 21:23–25), so proving its barbarity by comparison with the New. But is that necessarily so?

As has already been pointed out, the decree of Haman in 3:13 is reflected in that of Mordecai, and some of its wording is repeated in the later decree; but the differences also need to be taken into account. In 3:13 there is no doubt about the

---

[1] So L. B. Paton, *ICC*, p. 274; B. W. Anderson, *IB*, III, p. 866; C. A. Moore, *AB*, pp. 80 f. On the other hand L. E. Browne (*PCB*, p. 384) thinks it did not mean to authorize the Jews to murder the Persian women and children, 'though either interpretation is grammatically possible'.

meaning. The object of the verb *annihilate* follows immediately: 'all Jews, young and old, women and children'. In 8:11, on the other hand, the object of the verb is 'any armed force . . . that might attack', while 'them, with their children and women' is the object of the verb 'attack'.[1] This is the way in which NIV interprets the meaning, and indeed it is the plain sense of the text. Whatever ethical objection may be raised against the actions of the Jews as recorded in this book, at least they should not be based on this verse, misunderstood as it has commonly been.

**12.** *Upon one day.* Such killing was liable to escalate into an ongoing vendetta, but by specifying the date limits were set and the bloodshed contained.

**13.** On the word *copy* see comment on 3:14. It was not sufficient to publish the decree in writing; it would be proclaimed for all to hear. Instead of being defenceless the Jews were permitted to organize themselves to deal with any attack upon them and so *avenge themselves upon their enemies*, presuming that the Jews prevailed in the battle. This was justice, not revenge.

**14.** Emphasis is upon the haste with which the despatches were carried to their destinations, and in Susa there was no delay at all, for there the decree originated, in the heart of the royal citadel.

### c. The popularity of the Jews (8:15–17)

The final verses of the chapter are the antithesis of 3:14–15, where the effect of Haman's edict caused general consternation.

**15.** In the first place *the city* of Susa, and not merely the Jews living there, welcomed Mordecai as the prime minister. Far from resenting the appointment of a member of a foreign minority, the people cheered and rejoiced in full support. The distinctive robes in the royal colours and the *great golden crown* marked him out as second only to the king.[2]

---

[1] The verse is treated in some detail by Robert Gordis: 'Studies in the Esther Narrative' in *JBL* 95 (1976), pp. 49–53. He argues that 'them, their children and their wives, with their goods as booty' should be in inverted commas because these words are a citation from 3:13, indicating the original edict against which the Jews may now protect themselves.

[2] All the Hebrew words for 'crown' suggest by derivation a turban, coming as they do from verbs 'to surround'. C. A. Moore translates *ʿǎṭārâ* here 'turban' and points out that in the case of the crowns of the king and queen

**16**. The contrast between the reception of this decree and that of Haman was particularly marked among the Jews. In place of mourning, fasting, weeping and lamenting (4:3) there was *light and gladness and joy and honour*. The symbolic use of 'light' was already well established.

**17**. In the second place the provinces rejoiced when the edict reached them. The granting of a holiday implies that Gentile employers received the news with sympathetic understanding, and were willing to allow the Jews time for celebration. The fact that a Jew was directing affairs in the capital may have had something to do with the *fear of the Jews* that came over the empire. Mordecai had proved his ability to change what in theory could not be changed, and people were impressed as well as apprehensive for the future. Rightly sensing that it would in future be an advantage to be Jewish, many people *declared themselves Jews*. Only here in the Old Testament is reference made to people of other races becoming Jews, though the New Testament bears ample witness to the process in the first century AD (Mt. 23:15; Acts 2:10; 6:5; 13:43). True, the law had made provision for foreigners who lived in 'the land' (Lv. 19:33–34), and the prophets envisaged widespread conversion to the Lord from all over the earth (Is. 2:2–4; 49:6; Je. 3:17; Zp. 3:9; Zc. 8:22–23, to name but a few). But the verb used only here means 'they Judaized themselves', but by what process is not disclosed. The religion of the Jews had evidently become a separate issue from that of race.

Whereas chapter 3 had recorded the rise of Haman, this chapter has shown how Mordecai not only stepped into Haman's honoured role as the king's prime minister but also used his power in similar ways. The difference was that he worked more successfully and won popularity with Jews and Gentiles alike, and brought gladness instead of dismay.

---

(1:11; 2:17; 6:8) a different term (Heb. *keter*) is used. This latter word is confined to the book of Esther and probably represents a Persian original. The word *ʿtārâ* is once used in the Old Testament with the word 'bind' (Jb. 31:36), but elsewhere the context requires a metal crown (2 Sa. 12:30; Ps. 21:3 (4, Heb.); Zc. 6:11, 14). A. T. Olmstead makes several references to crowns, almost always of gold, but in a reference to a description of the goddess Anahita he writes, 'On her head she has *bound* a golden crown with a hundred stars of eight rays . . .' (*HPE*, p. 471, my italics). In Esther 8:15 the word 'coronet' would maintain the distinction from the royal crown and keep the right image; the evidence for 'turban' is scanty. See also P. Calmeyer, *Archäologische Mitteilungen aus Iran* 10 (1977), pp. 154–190 on the subject of crowns.

## Additional Note: 'Avenge, Avenge oneself, Vengeance' (Heb. *nāqam*)

For modern western readers of the book of Esther the most intractable problem is an ethical one, arising out of the very plot. How can Christians who take seriously the teaching of Jesus rejoice in the blood-bath into which the story develops? It has become part even of our cultural heritage to accept that enemies should be treated with kindness; as the sixteenth-century proverb says, 'The noblest vengeance is to forgive.' Moreover to avenge oneself, however justly, is uncivilized, and when indulged in by a group or society marks out a people as 'primitive'. History proves that such attempts to achieve a just settlement of a dispute lead at best to a cruel vendetta that may go on for generations, and at worst to protracted wars. By English law self-defence is therefore hedged about with so many restrictions that it becomes safest to assume that one has no right to use force or arms for self-defence, however great the provocations. It is necessary, however difficult we may find it, to realize that we bring our cultural conditioning to our reading of the biblical text in this case as in others, and consequently to make a conscious effort to understand the situation with which we are presented in this book.

But first it is helpful and interesting to see how our language has adopted two sets of words with a common origin. 'Avenge' and 'vengeance' came into English through French, which developed them from the Latin *vindicare*, but English also has the doublet 'vindicate', direct from Latin. The two are not entirely synonymous despite their common ancestry. Whereas the verb 'vindicate' has altogether commendable overtones, 'the good judge vindicates the right', 'avenge' and especially the noun 'vengeance' are associated with emotional reactions prompted by hatred. Inevitably the colour of words tends to influence our reading of them in whatever context they come, and that is certainly true here. It lies behind the note of one commentator on Esther 8:13, that the verb (avenge themselves) 'does not mean *to take vengeance* ... but *to inflict just punishment*'.[1] Unfortunately he does not justify this statement. More recently commentators have tended to assume the opposite to be the case, as for example Moore, who translates the

---

[1] Paul Haupt, *Critical Notes on Esther*, AJSLL 24 (1907–08), p. 161, author's italics; reprinted in C. A. Moore, *Studie in the Book of Esther*.

verb *take revenge*, 'the LXX has "fight against", which nicely eliminates the baser element of revenge'.[1] The essential question, however, is Hebrew usage as a pointer to the meaning in this context.

A study of the thirty or so verses of the Old Testament in which the verb is used shows that it does occur in contexts of personal revenge. Samson swore that he would be avenged upon the Philistines (Jdg. 15:7) and prayed to be able to carry out his desire (Jdg. 16:28). Saul also determined to avenge himself of the Philistines (1 Sa. 14:24; 18:25). Yet from the beginning this was shown to be contrary to the Lord's intention, and even Cain was divinely protected against violent death (Gn. 4:15). Lamech took advantage of the promise and reckoned he was safe, though he had unjustly taken life (Gn. 4:23–24). He is not heard of again! Indeed if a master so punished a slave that he or she died he was to 'suffer vengeance' (Ex. 21:20); the verb is used in a legal sense here.

On well over half the occasions when the verb is used the subject is the Lord God, or God gives instructions to his servants to carry out the sentence he has decreed. 'Vengeance is mine, and recompense . . . for the LORD will vindicate his people' (Dt. 32:35–36) are words Paul had in mind in Romans 12:19, and he went on to quote Proverbs 25:21–22, 'If your enemy is hungry, give him bread to eat . . .' The law of Leviticus 19:18, best known for its injunction to love our neighbours, also forbids vengeful feelings and grudges against others. So the law and popular wisdom taught the same truth, and the prophets took up the theme; the Lord was the avenger of wrongs, and because he was impartial Israel stood to suffer with the rest (Is. 1:24–25; Je. 5:9, 29; Ezk. 24:8; Na. 1:2). But once the punishment had been borne the nations which had inflicted it were themselves subject to the same law (Je. 50:15; 51:36; Ezk. 25:12, 15; *cf.* Lv. 26:25). Ideally, then, the Lord works out justice in the affairs of men and this is a cause for rejoicing not only for Israel but also for the nations (Dt. 32:43), whose authorities co-operate with God by executing God's wrath on the wrongdoer (Rom. 13:4b). The judge is called 'an avenger' (Gk. *ekdikos*; *cf. ekdikeō*, 'to procure justice for someone').

There was to be another way by which God would overcome evil, and it is hinted at in Psalm 8:2 (*cf.* Mt. 21:16, where our

---

[1] C. A. Moore, *AB*, p. 81.

Lord quotes it from LXX). Simply to praise God in his majesty was to set up a tower against an enemy, and so overcome him and still the avenger.

Old Testament usage makes one thing very clear, and that is that personal grievances were not to become the motivation for violent acts of vengeance. The Lord would avenge wrongs through the judges; but he was concerned for the whole of society as well as for the individual, and especially for the upholding of the covenant (Lv. 26:25), and while it was true that he heard the prayers of his people and forgave their sins, he was also 'an avenger of their wrongdoings' (Ps. 99:8). This warning provided a corrective to presumption and a safeguard against ruthlessness. Though in the book of Esther the tables had been turned on those who would have killed the Jews, the Jews had behind them all the theological conditioning provided by their scriptures, and their understanding of permission to avenge themselves would have been adjusted accordingly. Instead of having to endure slaughter without any means of self-defence, the new legislation permitted them to fight for one day against those who attacked them, and to kill them. The fact that this surprising change in the circumstances had taken place was awe-inspiring. It pointed to a providential ordering of their affairs, not to be taken lightly. To be sure it was wonderful, and a cause for rejoicing, but arrogance and presumption were ruled out, together with all bullying, self-assertive superiority, which in turn would call for God's condemnation and punishment.

The Christian injunction 'repay no one evil for evil' (Rom. 12:17), together with the positive 'overcome evil with good' (verse 21), remains the highest aim. Yet after all the years of Christian history a way of implementing this aim in national affairs still eludes us. That being so, any self-righteous, judgmental condemnation of Jewish action as contemplated in the decree of Esther 8 is misplaced. It is worth asking ourselves how we would react in the face of some devilish attack, aimed at exterminating our own nation. I suspect that we should not take it seriously, any more than we take the story of Esther as seriously as we ought. So much the worse for us. The Jewish people continue to have to live under such a threat.

# X. THE JEWS ARE SEEN TO TRIUMPH (9:1–19)

Only in the last two chapters of the book does the author reveal the reasons for some of his earlier allusions, and bring out his underlying intentions in writing the story of Esther. These chapters are therefore important for any appreciation of the book's purpose and its part in the total message of Scripture. In addition, of course, they work out the dénouement of the plot, so completing the story.

**1.** The deliberate and rather ponderous wording lays stress, first, on the exact date, already familiar from 3:12, and second, on the overturning of events so that the Jews, instead of being the victims, became the victors on that day. The outcome of the encounter is anticipated here as though the permission to defend themselves was certain to lead to their survival.

**2.** The inability of their enemies to do the Jews harm is explained on a psychological level: *the fear of them had fallen upon all peoples*. In part this fear could be explained by the unexpected change of power in Susa, and by the right of the Jews to defend themselves against a totally unjust law. People fighting in a just cause no doubt have formidable power, but none of these factors, nor all of them together, account for the implied inevitability of Jewish victory. The fear of God's people was explicable only in terms of fear of their God, who vindicated their righteous cause by convicting their enemies in the whole Persian empire of having backed the losing side.

**3.** That the highest authorities in every place had their eyes firmly fixed on political advantage for themselves is fully admitted. It was in their interests to ingratiate themselves with Mordecai if they were to remain in office, hence their readiness to help the Jews. With the leadership on their side the Jews secured powerful public support and even prestige.

**4.** Almost as mysterious as the fear of the Jews was the popularity of the new prime minister. Why should he have risen swiftly to such a powerful position in world politics, and why was it that people were prepared to trust him as their leader and champion his cause? A supernatural influence seems to be implied, enhancing natural tendencies to hero worship, and reinforcing self-interest.

**5–6.** Having explained how the Jews obtained favour, the author could go on to relate that they *smote all their enemies with the sword*. There are limits implied to the slaughter despite the emphasis on destruction. The victims were *i.* enemies, *ii.* those who hated them, *iii.* *men*, not women or children (Heb *'ĩš*). All the casualties are on one side in this battle, but we should think in terms of fighting men and not of a defenceless population as a whole, despite the many statements to the contrary in writings on Esther. Perhaps the words *did as they pleased to those who hated them* suggests an orgy of indulgence in elemental vengeance because of the juxtaposition of the verbs. In the wider context, however, the inference is that the Jews were given a free hand without official interference.[1] Human nature being what it is, to do one's pleasure often has grim overtones, as it does in Daniel 8:4; 11:3, 16, 36; but in Esther 1:8 it is morally neutral, while in Psalm 145 *God* satisfies the desire of every living thing (16, 19). The word translated 'pleasure', 'desire' (Heb. *raṣôn*) is neutral and does not of itself imply blame.

The number of casualties, however, was high. Five hundred in the acropolis of Susa seems excessive, and has even been taken as deliberate exaggeration for humorous effect. 'If an enemy did not attack the Jews first, he was in no danger. Who would be so foolish as to make himself subject to the second edict? It would be suicide to attack the Jews. . . . The answer is that 800 people in Susa and 75,000 in the provinces were so stupid! It is unfortunate that so many readers have failed to see that the account is a deliberate hyperbole.'[2] It is impossible to know what the death toll would have been if Haman's edict had been carried out, but there must have been ten times that number of Jews scattered throughout the Persian empire if the relatively small number who went back to Judah in the various waves of repatriation came to something like the figure of 42,360 (Ezr. 2:64; Ne. 7:66). Of course, those who argue for exaggeration in the cause of humour also consider Haman's edict to be exaggerated.

**7–10.** The killing of Haman's ten sons forestalled any attempt on their part to avenge the death of their father or to usurp the office he had held. Their names are spelt with

---

[1] Paul Haupt, writing in *AJSLL* in 1907–1908, commented, 'If the authorities had allowed the Jews to organize armed resistance, the numerous massacres in Russia during the past few years would have been nipped in the bud . . . But, as a rule, the assailants of the Russian Jews were supported by the governors, military commanders, officers of the police, etc.'

[2] Bruce W. Jones, 'Two Misconceptions about the Book of Esther', *CBQ* 39 (1977), p. 180.

considerable variations in the Versions and it is impossible to establish with certainty their original form, though claims have been made that Persian originals underlie at least some of them.[1] All the names have a characteristic 'a' vowel, in keeping also with the father and grandfather's names, as though binding the family together.

*But they laid no hand on the plunder.* In Israel's past there had been several incidents concerning spoils of war, and since the author makes this comment twice more (15 and 16) he clearly wants to make a point. This is especially likely in view of the express permission given to them in 8:11 to plunder the goods of their enemies. Abraham had refused to accept the spoil offered him by the king of Sodom (Gn. 14:21–23), so establishing a principle, and Saul had blatantly selected choice animals for himself while protesting his innocence, so providing a classic example of 'rationalization' and of the disaster that follows disobedience (1 Sa. 15:17–23). With the memory of this incident in mind the author seeks to reverse the curse on King Saul and ensure blessing for Mordecai and his contemporaries.[2] The deliberate decision not to enrich themselves at the expense of their enemies would not go unnoticed in a culture where victors were expected to take the spoil. The very novelty of such self-denial would be remarked upon and remembered, and taken as proof of the upright motives of the Jewish communities. The incident provides an interesting example of the way Scripture exerts its influence on behaviour.

What follows is less edifying, and not meant to be an example to follow, any more than was Saul's prevarication over the Amalekite animals (1 Sa. 15:13–15, 20–21).

**11–12.** At the end of the day the death-toll in the royal acropolis was reported to the king. By any standards to lose

[1] H. S. Gehman, 'Notes on the Persian Words in Esther', *JBL* 43 (1924), pp. 327f. He drew attention to the occurrence of *Parshandatha* (verse 7) on an ancient seal, now in the British Museum (Western Asiatic Antiquities, BM 89152). More recently Old Persian names have been recovered from the Persepolis administrative archives of 509–458 BC, from annotations on stone pestels and mortars, and from monuments, seals and coins. M. Mayrhofer, *Onomastica Persepolitana* (Vienna, 1973), has projected in many cases the Old Persian form, but lays stress on the fact that much remains unknown about Old Persian names. I am indebted to A. R. Millard of the School of Archaeology and Oriental Studies, University of Liverpool, for these and other details about Persian names.

[2] Berg, p. 67, explores this theme in some detail. As she points out, 'tne Jews honor the obligation ignored by their ancestors'.

500 men in one day was appalling, and there is a grim inference in the king's estimate of the total number killed in the rest of the king's provinces. That he should take it all so calmly, and go so far as to offer Esther a further attack on his fighting men, seems to Bruce Jones to accentuate the humorous element: 'The effect is almost slapstick: "If they have done that well in Susa, think what it must be like in the rest of the provinces!"' He may be right, but the narrator gives no hint of humour in his strictly factual report. The Jews were also citizens of the empire and potential soldiers; the king was subjecting his kingdom to even heavier loss when he permitted Haman's original edict, and perpetrated the initial injustice. Do Christian readers and commentators think it would have been better if the Jews had been subject to Haman's plot?

**13.** Presented with another *carte blanche* Esther shows no sign of weakening in her pursuit of local adversaries. So far the casualties had been in the acropolis, *Susa the capital* (11; *cf.* comment on 1:2), as opposed to the city, where most of the population was to be found. Esther's request is that a further day should be granted in which resistance there would be wiped out and the bodies of Haman's ten sons publicly exposed on gallows as a deterrent, as the bodies of Saul and his sons had been (1 Sa. 31:8–12).

**14.** So matter-of-fact is the reporting that the sequel tends to sound like cold-blooded cruelty. The king issued the decree and the rest followed.

**15.** *The Jews . . . gathered* refers back to 8:11 (*cf.* 9:2) and implies that troops remained in the city committed to carrying out the original edict. Only by organizing their men and arming them could resistance be effective. *On the fourteenth day of the month of Adar* (the date is of major importance to the author) the last defensive action was completed and Jewish safety from Haman's edict secured. Paton is of the opinion that this second day of killing was the author's way of explaining why there were two different dates for the observation of the feast of Purim in his day. 'History here arises from custom, not custom from history'.[1] This he must regard as self-evident, for he offers no supporting argument.

**16.** In the far-flung provinces of the empire also the drama was enacted, as other Jews *gathered to defend their lives* (again

[1]*ICC*, p. 288.

the same verb; *cf.* 9:15, note). They *got relief* from their enemies or 'rest' (AV, RV; Heb. *nôaḥ*), by killing a total of 75,000 opponents who would have killed them. Once more any temptation to gain material advantage out of the incident was resisted. Their enemies were welcome to the plunder.

**17.** Deliverance called for rejoicing, hence the institution of a holiday on the fourteenth of the month Adar, celebrated by feasting, one of the recurring themes of the book. Apart from the Feast of Dedication and Nicanor's Day, both instituted in the mid-second century BC, there were no festivals during the last five months of the Hebrew calendar (October to March). By the middle of the last month of the year a reason for family rejoicing would be a welcome highlight after the winter.

**18–19.** This first account of the institution of the festival points out the difference of practice between the date of the feast in Susa and that observed elsewhere. The reason for the difference has been accounted for in Esther's further request to the king (9:13); consequently Susa has to keep the fifteenth of Adar as the holiday, while everyone else keeps the fourteenth. As well as communal feasting there is an exchange of gifts, *choice portions* (*cf.* Ne. 8:12). Generous sharing both expressed gladness and increased it by ensuring that no-one was excluded by poverty from taking part. The narrative takes for granted the solidarity of the Jewish communities; scattered though they were over the empire, they kept their identity and rejoiced together in their common experience of deliverance. Thus a plot intended to destroy them resulted in a festival which helped to unite and sustain them as a people.

## XI. AUTHORITY FOR THE FESTIVAL (9:20–32)

These second and third accounts of the institution of Purim are commonly supposed to come from another writer, but quoted in order to complete the authentication of a feast which could not look to the Pentateuch for its definition and meaning. Nevertheless written documents with royal authority lay behind it.

**20.** Since the very continuation of the chosen race had been at stake, their rescue could not but be commemorated. *Mordecai recorded these things*, that is the events of the previous section, as they concerned all the Jewish people, incorporating the important aspects in letters which gave a directive for the future. The fact that the royal postal system had been set up, and that Mordecai in his official capacity as prime minister had the right to make use of it, made communication relatively easy and comprehensive, reaching *all the Jews . . . both near and far*. Distances of up to 2,000 miles could have been involved.

**21-22**. First the date of the feast needed to be established, and Mordecai decreed that both the fourteenth and fifteenth of Adar should be observed annually. Future generations would be given an annual reminder of the wonderful deliverance from extinction: sorrow turned to joy and mourning into celebration.[1] Mordecai now specifies that the festivities should include *gifts to the poor* as well as the exchange of presents (19).

**23-28**. The third account of the institution of the feast explains how it got its name, Purim. Of necessity part of the story has to be retold.

**24**. This summary of Haman's decision to plot against the Jews, and in order to find the most propitious day to cast lots so that he would be sure to succeed, links the derivation of Purim with the word *pûr* (*cf.* verse 26), 'lot'. The translation was essential because the word was not Hebrew, and many suggestions have been made as to its origin. The argument was thought to have been settled by Julius Levy.[2] He argued in favour of its derivation from the Babylonian *pūru*, 'stone', but it is now known that the 'lot' could be of wood or stone, and the derivation is doubtful. The finding of 'the die of Iahali', bearing the word *pūru*, has both settled the question of derivation and shed light on the importance attached to auspicious dates in Persia.[3] The lot was used in Assyria for choosing annual eponym officials, dividing property and in divination, and the practice lived on in the eastern part of the empire in Persian times.

**25**. *But when Esther came before the king* is literally 'when she came'. RSV represents a traditional interpretation of the writer's meaning (*cf.* AV), but the pronoun 'she' could refer to a feminine noun, hence 'but when the plot came to the king's attention' (NIV). Since Esther's name had not been mentioned

---

[1] Though the New Testament writers do not quote from the book of Esther, there may be an allusion to this chapter, with its repetition of the word 'rest', in 2 Thes. 1:7, where relief from persecution is the context.

[2] *HUCA* 14 (1939), p. 144.

[3] See Introduction II. *c.* 'Purim', and W. W. Hallo, 'The First Purim', *BA* 46.1 (1983), p. 22; W. von Soden, *Akkadisches Handwörterbuch II* (1972), pp. 881-882 *sub pūru*. He gives references to the lot from Sumerian (*c.* 19th century to 6th century BC).

in connection with Mordecai's letters, the latter translation is to be preferred. Mordecai was concerned more with instituting the festival than with perpetuating his own or Esther's part in events, and incidentally the king is credited with carrying out just punishment on the guilty Haman and his sons, without anyone's intervention. That Esther had put the ideas into the king's mind was a secondary matter which did not need to be dwelt upon in the letter.

**26.** The letter did no more than reinforce and regulate what Jewish people everywhere had begun spontaneously to practise (verse 19). The festival arose out of relief and thanksgiving at their deliverance.

**27–28.** Given the lead of Mordecai, there was ready acceptance of *these two days*, and his contemporaries committed *their descendants and all who joined them*, a reference to the fact that a certain number of Gentiles were drawn to the worship of God and so to the Jewish communities (8:17), to observance of the dates in every place and for all time. So comprehensive and emphatic is the statement of these verses that some commentators have suggested that the book may at one stage in its development have ended here, and that verse 28 would have made a suitable ending for the story. It seems more likely that the passage from which the quotation came, if indeed it is a quotation (*cf.* p. 107), ended at this point. The threat which had been intended to annihilate the Jewish race became an occasion for uniting it, and Purim, like the other communal feasts, undoubtedly played its part in Jewish survival through the centuries in scattered geographical areas of Europe, Asia and Africa, because it kept Jews apart from other people by its distinctiveness.

**29–32.** Further official authority is cited for the festival. This time Queen Esther adds her royal command and joins Mordecai in writing official letters.

These last four verses of the chapter appear at first sight to be an unnecessary duplication of what has gone before, but a tradition commemorating deliverance from death is the author's goal and he does not hesitate to add yet more evidence in order to reinforce the importance for the Jews of keeping the annual festival.[1] In these verses Esther plays the leading role, having last been mentioned in verse 13. She now

---

[1] Grounds for thinking that these verses are secondary, *i.e.* not part of the original, are considered in detail by Samuel E. Loewenstamm, 'Esther 9:29–32: The Genesis of a Late Addition' in *HUCA* 42 (1971), pp. 117–124.

appears as legislator, her royal authority bringing to a climax an ascending scale of good reasons why the days of Purim should be observed.

**29**. Use of official names and mention of written documents make it reasonable to suppose that the author may have been drawing on legal material here. It is interesting to note that whereas Mordecai is called 'the Jew', Esther, who might have been so designated, is given her patronym. Was it considered advantageous to play down the descent of the queen from foreign stock?

Despite the plural subject the first word of the verse in Hebrew is a feminine singular verb, indicating that Esther is the effective subject: 'she decreed'. Mention of Mordecai brings out the connection between his legislation and that of the queen, but nevertheless it is grammatically problematic. A complicating factor is uncertainty over the meaning of the word *toqep̄*, a rare word translated 'power' in 10:2 and in Daniel 11:17, the only other place in the Old Testament where the noun occurs. *Gave full written authority* captures the sense well; NIV, by putting 'along with Mordecai the Jew' in parenthesis, also makes Queen Esther the subject of the verb.[1] *Full written authority* shows how important by this time written documents were held to be throughout the empire. The very fact that they were written gave permanence and a kind of independent identity (*cf.* Gk. *gegraptai*, 'it stands written', in LXX. *E.g.* Ezr. 3:2; Ne. 10:34; in the Gospels Mt. 4:4, 6, 10).

**30**. *Letters . . . in words of peace and truth* is a strange turn of phrase which has given rise to some discussion. Robert Gordis has argued that it is a reference to the formal words of greeting with which letters customarily began, and frequently still do, in Hebrew.[2] The writer omitted the contents of the letter because its subject-matter was already well known. Sandra Beth Berg, on the other hand, points out that in the Hebrew the last words of the next verse (verse 31) contain a similarly

---

[1]Loewenstamm (*art. cit.*, p. 119) argues that *toqep̄* means a 'deed of legal strength', but since he goes on to say 'It seems that neither the Septuagint nor the last redactor of MT was still aware of the fact that *tqp̄* had this special meaning' (p. 120), doubt is cast on his thesis, especially as the same word is used with the meaning 'strength' in such close proximity as 10:2.

[2]'Studies in the Esther Narrative' in *JBL* 95.1 (March 1976). pp. 57f. From an exhaustive analysis J. A. Fitzmyer ('Some Notes on Aramaic Epistolography', *JBL* 95.1 (1974), pp. 201–225) finds the word 'peace' used in the vast majority of greetings, whereas 'truth' features neither in opening nor in concluding formulae.

constructed expression 'words of fasting and supplication'.[1] In view of the fact that the latter phrase refers to the contents of legislation, she argues that the same is probably true of the similar words in verse 30. The juxtaposition of peace (Heb. *šālôm*) and truth (Heb. *ʾemet*) first occurs in connection with Hezekiah (2 Ki. 19; *cf.* Is. 39:8: 'There will be peace and security in my days'). The same two Hebrew words in Jeremiah 33:6 are translated 'prosperity and security' (RSV) and in Zechariah 8:16, where they occur in the opposite order, 'true and sound judgment' (NIV). Such usage shows how wide ranging were the concepts behind these two words. Celebration of Purim commemorated the overthrow of evil designs and the vindication of the innocent; by the annual reminder of the triumph of justice over wrongdoing true and right dealing in the community would be encouraged, security would be promoted and the cause of peace advanced.

**31.** Because the festival would have such beneficial effects Esther and Mordecai committed themselves and their descendants to its observance, but only here since chapter 4 are *their fasts and their lamenting* referred to. The word *lamenting* (Heb. root *zʿq*) means basically 'cry out', usually in distress (*cf.* 4:1) and often in prayer to God (*e.g.* Ne. 9:4, 28), hence the translation 'supplication'. It seems unlikely that fasting became part of the annual commemoration at that time, though a fast was observed by the Jews at Purim in the mediaeval period. Nevertheless fasting is a major theme of the book, so there is good reason for expecting that it would feature in the recapitulation of the concluding section, at least in passing. As Sandra Beth Berg observes, 'Even if 9:29–32 stems from a later hand, its author is sensitive to the style and spirit of the tale.'[2]

**32.** A similar stylistic feature which points to unity of authorship is the word *command* (Heb. *maʾamar*). This particular formation, from *ʾāmar*, 'to speak, promise, command', occurs in the Old Testament only in the book of Esther (1:15; 2:20). In view of the fact that it is a rare word its use in 1:15 does appear to point to a deliberate comparison between 'the command of King Ahasuerus' there and 'the command of Queen Esther' here. To quote the same passage from Sandra Beth Berg, 'Some consideration should be devoted to internal evidence, prior to excising these verses as secondary.'

[1]Berg, p. 44.    [2]Berg, p. 38.

## ADDITIONAL NOTE: PORTIONS

The introduction of Queen Esther in verses 29–32 provides royal assent to the law-making of Mordecai, whereupon the legislation presumably was added to all the rest of the laws of the Medes and Persians, which could not be repealed. *It was recorded in writing* is literally 'in the book'. C. A. Moore prefers 'in a book', so emending the text, but the phrase could well have had adverbial status, indicating its fixed and authoritative form.

## Additional Note: Portions (Heb. *meⁿôṯ*)

The author of the book of Esther chooses his words with care and makes sure they do his bidding. He often introduces an unusual word more than once, so drawing attention to its special place in his scheme. Such a word with particular significance is 'portions'.

Within the book of Esther the idea occurs twice, first in connection with Hegai's special interest in Esther as a likely candidate to become the new queen (2:9), and secondly in describing the observance of Purim (9:19, 22), but the theme (though not the same Hebrew word) occurs already in the Joseph narrative (Gn. 43:34), where it indicates that his brothers are receiving honoured attentions. Similarly Daniel and his friends were honoured by Nebuchadrezzar by gifts of the king's rich food, and later in the exile King Jehoiachin dined at the king's table and received 'every day a portion, as long as he lived' (2 Ki. 25:30). The practice thus extended at least from Egypt to Persia over many centuries (*cf.* also 1 Sa. 9:22–24).

The English word 'portion' is far too colourless to capture the emotional content evident, for instance, in Joseph's presents to his brothers, and to a lesser extent in the other contexts. The child who comes back from a party with a tasty morsel and says, 'I saved this for you', is near to capturing the spirit of the ancient love-gift, and there are still many cultures in which those privileged to attend a feast expect, and are expected, to take back home, to those who could not attend, some token from the banquet. This is the joyous spirit prompting the words 'send portions to him for whom nothing is prepared' at the time of Ezra's reading from the law book (Ne. 8:10).

There is, however, another context in which the word acquired a different connotation, and that is in connection with sacrifices and the portions of the animals allocated to different Temple groups (2 Ch. 31:4; Ne. 12:44, 47; 13:10). It is not a long step from this use of the word to the believer's conviction that his portion is the Lord (Ps. 16:5), and by contrast to the unwelcome portion of those who consistently choose evil (Je. 13:25). Psalm 16 goes on to elaborate on the lot (Heb. *gôrāl*) which is in the Lord's hand, and the psalmist comments,

> The lines have fallen for me in pleasant places;
> yea, I have a goodly heritage (Ps. 16:6).

Here the 'lot' or 'portion' is an allusion to the way life has worked out; the psalmist is thinking of all the signs of God's providence which have marked his pilgrimage, and which unbelievers think of as 'fate'. It would not be surprising, therefore, if the word had within it suggestions of destiny. 'Within the context of Esther's receipt of portions from Hegai, the special favor she receives anticipates the king's later reaction to her. This, in turn, results in Esther's coronation feast (2:18).'[1] At the end of the story, when festivities mark the reversal of Jewish fortunes from the threat of death to life and favour, the exchange of 'portions' is especially appropriate. The sending of 'portions' often signified special favour, 'and sending portions in observance of Purim symbolizes the privileged status of the Jews in Ahasuerus' empire. This status is attained through the reversal of the Jews' *gôrāl* [lot]. Sending portions, then, suitably characterizes the celebration of the feast of "lots".'[2]

Such stylistic use of language easily passes the modern reader by, and yet it is characteristic of Hebrew writing. The New Testament writers also, steeped as they are in the Scriptures of the Old Testament, make use of the LXX in similarly allusive ways.[3] To miss the allusions and their significance may lead to misinterpretation of the text.

The use of this unusual word at the beginning and the end

[1]Berg, p. 45.   [2]Berg, p. 46.
[3]See, for example, Marjorie Warkentin, *Ordination: A Biblical-historical View* (Eerdmans, Grand Rapids, 1982). 'The Bible of the early Christians was the Septuagint. Paul and Luke use the vocabulary of this version for purposes of recall and association of ideas. ... The laying on of hands in the New Testament must be evaluated in conjunction with its Old Testament connections' (p. 155).

of the story contributes to the evidence for unity of authorship More than that, it shows that the writer saw Purim in terms of God's favour to Esther, and through her to his people. Purim celebrates the miracle of deliverance, not the bloodshed it entailed, and that is why it was suitably commemorated in the exchange of love-gifts and in communal feasting.

## XII. NORMAL LIFE RESTORED (10:1–3)

The book began with King Ahasuerus and now finishes with a brief reference to him as his reign impinged on the life of the ordinary citizen, especially in the far-flung countries of the empire.

**1.** Quality of life for the common people depended not only on the harvests but also on the degree of taxation demanded by the royal purse for civil and military projects, as well as for supplies of food and other resources to keep the palace and the civil service in luxury. The simple statement *King Ahasuerus laid tribute on . . .* is charged with meaning. In the Old Testament *tribute* (Heb. *mas*) usually means conscription to forced labour (*e.g.* 1 Ki: 5:13 (5:27, Heb.)). In the Persian period it could still have this connotation, but the use of money by this time had made possible taxation in coinage as well as in kind, so giving the word coverage of all these means of exacting benefit. *On the land and on the coastlands of the sea* implies the king's ownership of all this territory, the coasts being the eastern Mediterranean generally, with its many islands.

Though distant, these cultured regions were a source of wealth which successive conquerors exploited to the full. Over-taxation was a feature of life in the provinces, whereas, according to Olmstead, Persia itself had long since ceased to pay taxes.[1] In the time-honoured method each province had to provide supplies for the ruler during a fixed period each year (*cf.* 1 Ki. 4:7); Babylonia, for example, had to be responsible for four months out of every twelve, apart from normal tribute, the whole of the rest of Asia being responsible for the remaining eight.[2] The necessity of contributing these supplies imposed a heavy burden and tended to keep the population of the provinces impoverished. The laconic reference, therefore, to the king and his tribute would have been sufficient to

[1]*HPE*, p. 291.    [2]Herodotus, *The Histories* i. 193. *Cf.* 1 Ki. 4:22–28.

conjure up for contemporaries the daily anxieties of making ends meet, but without in any way implying disloyalty to the sovereign.

**2.** The reader's attention is drawn rather to a source of further information from which the king's prestige will be further enhanced. The reference to *the Book of the Chronicles of the kings of Media and Persia* is in line with many such in the biblical books of Kings and Chronicles, when older authorities are cited (*e.g.* 1 Ki. 14:19; 15:7, 23, 31; 1 Ch. 27:24). The question is whether the reference here is to an official court history in the Persian archives or to a Jewish record, to which access would be more easily obtained. On the whole the latter seems more likely, though if Mordecai was second only to the king it is inconceivable that his name would not have appeared in the official account of the reign of Ahasuerus.[1] The references in 2:23 and 6:1 are, to judge from the context, to a kind of daily account of events at court, rather than to official history, as here. *Media and Persia* names the two kingdoms in chronological order (*cf.* Dn. 8:20), suggesting perhaps an account covering several centuries. When our author put Persia before Media (1:3, 18) he was accurately reflecting the supremacy of Persia in his day.

**3.** Miraculously the power behind the throne of this mighty empire was a Jew and therefore, though this is not spelt out, one who feared God and stood for justice and right in the affairs of state. Who would have expected that the exiled Jews would ever have a representative in so influential a position? He could be counted on to protect them against exploitation and any further attempts during his lifetime to exterminate them. His interest was not in promoting his own advantage but the *welfare* (Heb. *ṭôḇ* 'good') of the whole Jewish community, and he *spoke peace* (Heb. *šālôm*), which means prosperity of all kinds, health, security, material plenty and good relationships.[2] In making these his aims for the total Israelite population of the empire he would secure prosperity also for the countries as a whole. Such an effective leader was likely to be popular and revered, not only by his own people but also by the population at large.

Through the defeat of Haman's evil intentions the whole

---

[1] For a contrary view see *AB*, p. 99.

[2] On the use of the term *šālôm* in connection with diplomatic settlement of differences see D. J. Wiseman, ' "Is it peace?" – Covenant and Diplomacy', *VT* XXXII. 3 (1982), pp. 311–326.

empire had entered a period of peace and well-being, blessed through the descendants of Abraham (Gn. 12:3), though still more profound blessings were part of the purpose of the far-reaching prophecy.

## Additional Note: Esther and Jewry

In the course of the commentary a connection has been assumed between the deliverance of the Jews in the time of Esther and the events of the last hundred years which have culminated in their return to Palestine. The purpose of this note is to comment upon this assumption and, at the risk of oversimplification, to pursue some of its implications.

Whereas most of the nations that surrounded pre-exilic Israel lost their identity long ago, the Jews (as they came to be known from the name of their state of Judah after the exile) have maintained themselves through all the intervening centuries as a distinguishable people, while living as foreigners in Europe, N. Africa and W. Asia. Throughout their history they have felt a strong attachment to 'the land', kept alive by the cry of hope used at Passover, 'Next year in Jerusalem' and by daily liturgical prayers for a return to that city. 'Equally impressive is the unbroken contact which the Jews of the Dispersion maintained with the land of Palestine, and that, not only as a place of pious pilgrimage but as a continuing centre of Jewish life. . . . From Palestine in the grim period after the destruction of Jerusalem came the Mishnah and from Palestine also, some five hundred years later, came the Massoretic text of the Hebrew Scriptures.'[1] Jewish communities continued to live in Palestine, despite the campaigns of the Crusaders and the subsequent Muslim rule, and were joined periodically by Jews from other countries whose lives had been made intolerable by persecution. Partly as a result of the contribution made by those who returned to Palestine, the Jewish community there was revitalized. 'When in the nineteenth century the Jews began to look for somewhere to live in safety, Palestine was the only country which could stir the general interest.'[2] This was the country they believed to be their homeland, and to which they looked as the origin of

[1]Denys Baly, *Multitudes in the Valley, Church and Crisis in the Middle East* (Seabury Press, New York, 1957), p. 22. Quoted by Colin Chapman, *Whose Promised Land?* (Lion Publishing, 1983), p. 35.
[2]Denys Baly, quoted in Colin Chapman, *Whose Promised Land?*, p. 36.

all they held dear.

Recurring festivals, observance of the sabbath and circumcision will all have played their part in sustaining the Jewish people over the centuries, but Purim, with its obligatory reading of Esther in the family circle, will have been particularly influential in maintaining hope in the future of their people. The book of Esther illustrated only too clearly the threat under which Jewish communities lived when they were subject to foreign kings and on foreign soil, and so, though the book made no explicit mention of Judah or Jerusalem, implicitly it would encourage hopes of a life of freedom in their own land, where their religion could be practised without fear.

The establishment of the Jewish homeland, especially in the light of the long centuries of suffering and homelessness endured by the Jews, deserves to be viewed sympathetically even on humanitarian grounds, and yet, in the process of finding homes for returning Jews, other people, similarly convinced that they had a right to live in Palestine, had to be displaced, or live (as many Arabs do) under Israeli rule. We have argued that the outcome of Haman's plot proved that God's providence was at work to vindicate the right through Mordecai and Esther. The hand of God can no less have been at work to order the long series of events that brought the Jews to the land of Palestine again. That does not necessarily mean, however, that all is as God would have it be, that there have been no injustices committed, and that in the affairs of the nation God's word is normative. Some of Israel's greatest spokesmen see the establishment of the state as a step backwards rather than forwards, because 'the same biological and racist arguments extended by the Nazis, and which inspired the inflammatory laws of Nuremberg, serve as the basis for the official definition of Jewishness in the bosom of the state of Israel'.[1] There are other anomalies. One Rabbi Yosef Becher explains that he and other rabbis were against a Jewish state because it was 'not the will of the Almighty'.[2] He regards the

[1]Haim Cohen, a judge of the Supreme Court of Israel, quoted by Colin Chapman, *Whose Promised Land?*, p. 192. This book examines the claims and counter-claims to the 'promised land' and looks again at the Bible and its promises. It gives different points of view in the words of those holding them, as well as the judgment of one who has faced the issues first hand. See also R. T. France, 'Old Testament Prophecy and the Future of Israel', *Tyndale Bulletin* 26 (1975), pp. 53–78.

[2]Colin Chapman, *Whose Promised Land?*, p. 193.

state as temporary. So it is not only disinterested observers who regret the bitter polarization that has arisen between Arab and Jew, giving rise to further oppression and suffering.

Whatever may be said in defence of Esther's request for further bloodshed in Susa on the fourteenth of the month Adar (Est. 9:11–15), that also strikes most commentators as excessive and reprehensible. It is none the less true to human history. If the threat to the Jews had not been made in the first place there would have been no occasion for the killings. In the recent events it was anti-Semitism on the part of so-called Christian nations that gave rise to Zionism, for if the Jews had been allowed to live in peace among them there would have been no reason for militancy. When those who have been oppressed find themselves with power they rarely exercise restraint. Popular opinion even asks, 'Why should they?', and yet at the same time decries cruelty and loss of life. It is difficult to see, in the light of such incompatible opinions, how a coherent judgment of what is just can be achieved.

The biblical evidence points to God's purpose in preserving the Jewish nation from extinction, in Egypt, in Babylon and in Persia. In the broadest terms it was because that nation was being prepared for the honour of receiving his Son. Queen Esther in her day fulfilled her part in saving the nation from destruction. Once Jesus had come God's purpose to gather together all things in Christ became operative (Gal. 3:28–29). Hard though it is for Arabs and Jews to accept this truth from Christians, only in Christ will God's promise to Abraham be fulfilled: 'in thee shall all the families of the earth be blessed' (Gn. 12:3, AV).

# APPENDIX

## THE GREEK ADDITIONS[1]

**A.**

*In the second year of the reign of the great King Ahasuerus, on the first day of Nisan, a dream came to Mordecai son of Jair, son of Shimei, son of Kish, of the tribe of Benjamin, a Jew living at Susa and holding high office at the royal court. He was one of the captives whom Nebuchadnezzar, king of Babylon, had deported from Jerusalem with Jeconiah, king of Judah.*

*This was his dream. There were cries and noise, thunder and earthquakes, and disorder over the whole earth. Then two great dragons came forward, each ready for the fray, and set up a great roar. At the sound of them every nation made ready to wage war against the nation of the just. A day of darkness and gloom, of affliction and distress, oppression and great disturbance on earth! The righteous nation was thrown into consternation at the fear of the evils awaiting them, and prepared for death, crying out to God. Then from their cry, as from a little spring, there grew a great river, a flood of water. Light came as the sun rose, and the humble were raised up and devoured the mighty.*

*On awakening from this dream and vision of God's designs, Mordecai thought deeply on the matter, trying his best all day to discover what its meaning might be.*

*Lodging at court with Bigthan and Teresh, two of the king's eunuchs who guarded the palace, Mordecai got wind of their intentions and uncovered their plot. Learning that they were preparing to assassinate King Ahasuerus, he warned the king against them. The king gave orders for the two eunuchs to be tortured; they confessed and were executed. The king then had these events recorded in his Chronicles, while Mordecai himself also wrote an account of them. The king then appointed Mordecai to an office at court and rewarded him with presents. But Haman son of Hammedatha, the Agagite, who enjoyed high favour*

[1]See Introduction, VI. 3, pp. 45–47, above. The text is taken from The Jerusalem Bible, published and copyright 1966, 1967 and 1968 by Darton, Longman & Todd Ltd and Doubleday & Co. Inc., and is used by permission of the publishers.

*with the king, determined to injure Mordecai in revenge for the king's two eunuchs.*

## B.

*The text of the letter was as follows:*

'The great King, Ahasuerus, to the governors of the hundred and twenty-seven provinces stretching from India to Ethiopia, and to their subordinate district commissioners.

'Being placed in authority over many nations and ruling the whole world, I have resolved never to be carried away by the insolence of power, but always to rule with moderation and clemency, so as to assure for my subjects a life ever free from storms and, offering my kingdom the benefits of civilisation and free transit from end to end, to restore that peace which all men desire. In consultation with our advisers as to how this aim is to be effected, we have been informed by one of them, eminent among us for prudence and well proved for his unfailing devotion and unshakeable trustworthiness, and in rank second only to our majesty, Haman by name, that there is, mingled among all the tribes of the earth a certain ill-disposed people, opposed by its laws to every other nation and continually defying the royal ordinances, in such a way as to obstruct that form of government assured by us to the general good.

'Considering therefore that this people, unique of its kind, is in complete opposition to all mankind from which it differs by its outlandish system of laws, that it is hostile to our interests and that it commits the most heinous crimes, to the point of endangering the stability of the realm:

'We command that the people designated to you in the letters written by Haman, appointed to watch over our interests and a second father to us, are all, including women and children, to be destroyed root and branch by the swords of their enemies, without any pity or mercy, on the fourteenth day of the twelfth month, Adar, of the present year, so that, these past and present malcontents being in one day forcibly thrown down to Hades, our government may henceforward enjoy perpetual stability and peace.'

## C.

### Mordecai's prayer

*Then calling to mind all the wonderful works of the Lord, he offered this prayer:*

*'Lord, Lord, King and Master of all things,*
*everything is subject to your power,*
*and there is no one who can withstand you*
*in your will to save Israel.*

*'Yes, you have made heaven and earth,*
*and all the marvels that are under heaven.*
*You are the Lord of all,*
*and there is none who can resist you, Lord.*

*'You know all things;*
*you know, Lord, you know,*
*that no insolence, arrogance, vainglory*
*prompted me to this,*
*to this refusal to bow down*
*before proud Haman.*
*I would readily have kissed his feet*
*for the safety of Israel.*

*'But what I did, I did*
*rather than place the glory of a man*
*above the glory of God;*
*and I will not bow down to any*
*but to you, Lord;*
*in so refusing I will not act in pride.*

*'And now, Lord God,*
*King, God of Abraham,*
*spare your people!*
*For men are seeking our ruin*
*and plan to destroy your ancient heritage.*
*Do not overlook your inheritance,*
*which you redeemed for your own out of the land of Egypt.*
*Hear my supplication,*
*have mercy on your heritage,*
*and turn our grief into rejoicing,*
*that we may live to hymn your name, Lord.*
*Do not suffer the mouths*
*of those who praise you to perish.'*

*And all Israel cried out with all their might, for they were faced with death.*

## Esther's prayer

*Queen Esther also took refuge with the Lord in the mortal peril which had overtaken her. She took off her sumptuous robes and put on sorrowful mourning. Instead of expensive perfumes she covered her head with ashes and dung. She humbled her body severely, and the former scenes of her happiness and elegance were now littered with tresses torn from her hair. She besought the Lord God of Israel in these words:*

'My Lord, our King, the only one,
come to my help, for I am alone
and have no helper but you
and am about to take my life in my hands.

'I have been taught from my earliest years, in the bosom of my family,
that you, Lord, chose
Israel out of all the nations
and our ancestors out of all the people of old times
to be your heritage for ever;
and that you have treated them as you promised.

'But then we sinned against you,
and you handed us over to our enemies
for paying honour to their gods.
Lord, you are just.

'But even now they are not satisfied
with the bitterness of our slavery:
they have put their hands in the hands of their idols
to abolish the decree that your own lips have uttered,
to blot out your heritage,
to stop the mouths of those who praise you,
to quench your altar and the glory of your House,
and instead to open the mouths of the heathen,
to sing the praise of worthless idols
and forever to idolise a king of flesh.

'Do not yield your sceptre, Lord,
to non-existent beings.
Never let men mock at our ruin.
Turn their designs against themselves,
and make an example of him who leads the attack on us.
Remember, Lord; reveal yourself
in the time of our distress.

*'As for me, give me courage,*
*King of gods and master of all power.*
*Put persuasive words into my mouth*
*when I face the lion;*
*change his feeling into hatred for our enemy,*
*that the latter and all like him may be brought to their end.*

*'As for ourselves, save us by your hand,*
*and come to my help, for I am alone*
*and have no one but you, Lord.*
*You have knowledge of all things,*
*and you know that I hate honours from the godless,*
*that I loathe the bed of the uncircumcised,*
*of any foreigner whatever.*
*You know I am under constraint,*
*that I loathe the symbol of my high position*
*bound round my brow when I appear at court;*
*I loathe it as if it were a filthy rag*
*and do not wear it on my days of leisure.*
*Your handmaid has not eaten at Haman's table,*
*nor taken pleasure in the royal banquets,*
*nor drunk the wine of libations.*
*Nor has your handmaid found pleasure*
*from the day of her promotion until now*
*except in you, Lord, God of Abraham.*
*O God, whose strength prevails over all,*
*listen to the voice of the desperate,*
*save us from the hand of the wicked,*
*and free me from my fear.'*

## D.

On the third day, *when she had finished praying, she took off her suppliant's mourning attire* and dressed herself in her full splendour. *Radiant as she then appeared, she invoked God who watches over all men and saves them. Then she took two maids with her. With a delicate air she leaned on one, while the other accompanied her carrying her train. She leaned on the maid's arm as though languidly, but in fact because her body was too weak to support her; the other maid followed her mistress, lifting her robes which swept the ground. Rosy with the full flush of her beauty, her face radiated joy and love; but her heart shrank with fear.* Having passed through door after door, she found herself in the presence of the king. He was seated

123

on the royal throne, *dressed in all his robes of state, glittering with gold and precious stones – a formidable sight.* Raising his face, *afire with majesty, he looked on her, blazing with anger. The queen sank down. She grew faint and the colour drained from her face, and she leaned her head against the maid who accompanied her. But God changed the king's heart,* inducing a milder spirit. *He sprang from his throne in alarm and took her in his arms until she recovered, comforting her with soothing words. 'What is the matter, Esther?'* he said *'I am your brother. Take heart; you will not die; our order only applies to ordinary people. Come to me.'* And raising his golden sceptre he laid it on her neck, *embraced her and said, 'Speak to me'. 'My lord,'* she said *'you looked to me like an angel of God, and my heart was moved with fear of your majesty. For you are a figure of wonder, my lord, and your face is full of graciousness.' But as she spoke she fell down in a faint. The king was distressed, and all his attendants tried their best to revive her.*

## E.

*The text of the letter was as follows:*

'The great King, Ahasuerus, to the satraps of the hundred and twenty-seven provinces which stretch from India to Ethiopia, to the provincial governors and to all our loyal subjects, greeting.

'Many men, repeatedly honoured by the extreme bounty ·of their benefactors, only grow the more arrogant. It is not enough for them to seek our subjects' injury, but unable as they are to support the weight of their own surfeit they turn to scheming against their benefactors themselves. Not content with banishing gratitude from the human heart, but elated by the plaudits of men unacquainted with goodness, notwithstanding that all is for ever under the eye of God, they vainly expect to escape his justice, so hostile to the wicked. Thus it has often happened to those placed in authority that, having entrusted friends with the conduct of affairs and allowed themselves to be influenced by them, they find themselves sharing with these the guilt of innocent blood and involved in irremediable misfortunes, the upright intentions of rulers having been misled by false arguments of the evilly disposed. This may be seen without recourse to the history of earlier times to which we have referred; you have only to look at what is before you, at the crimes perpetrated by a plague of unworthy officials. For the future we will exert our efforts to assure the tranquillity and peace of the realm for all, by adopting new policies and by always judging matters that are brought to our notice in the most equitable spirit.

'Thus Haman son of Hammedatha, a Macedonian, without a drop

*of Persian blood and far removed from our goodness, enjoyed our hospitality and was treated by us with the benevolence which we show to every nation, even to the extent of being proclaimed our 'father' and being accorded universally the prostration of respect as second in dignity to the royal throne. But he, unable to keep within his own high rank, schemed to deprive us of our realm and of our life. Furthermore, by tortuous wiles and arguments, he would have had us destroy Mordecai, our saviour and constant benefactor, with Esther the blameless partner of our majesty, and their whole nation besides. He thought by these means to leave us without support and so to transfer the Persian empire to the Macedonians.*

'*But we find that the Jews, marked out for annihilation by this arch-scoundrel, are not criminals: they are in fact governed by the most just of laws. They are sons of the Most High, the great and living God to whom we and our ancestors owe the continuing prosperity of our realm. You will therefore do well not to act on the letter sent by Haman son of Hammedatha, since their author has been hanged at the gates of Susa with his whole household: a well-earned punishment which God, the ruler of all things, has speedily inflicted on him. Put up copies of this letter everywhere, allow the Jews freedom to observe their own customs, and come to their help against anyone who attacks them on the day originally chosen for their maltreatment, that is the thirteenth day of the twelfth month, which is Adar. For the all-powerful God has made this day a day of joy and not of ruin for his chosen people. Jews, for your part, among your solemn festivals celebrate this as a special day with every kind of feasting, so that now and in the future, for you and for Persians of good will it may commemorate your rescue, and for your enemies may stand as a reminder of their ruin.*

'*Every city and, more generally, every country, which does not follow these instructions, will be mercilessly devastated with fire and sword, and made not only inaccessible to men but hateful to wild animals and even birds for ever.*'

**F.**
*And Mordecai said, 'All this is God's doing. I remember the dream I had about these matters, nothing of which has failed to come true: the little spring that became a river, the light that shone, the sun, the flood of water. Esther is the river – she whom the king married and made queen. The two dragons are Haman and myself. The nations are those that banded together to blot out the name of Jew. The single nation, mine, is Israel, those who cried out to God and were saved. Yes, the Lord has saved his people, the Lord has delivered us from all these*

evils, God has worked such signs and great wonders as have never happened among the nations.

'Two destinies he appointed, one for his own people, one for the nations at large. And these two destinies were worked out at the hour and time and day laid down by God involving all the nations. In this way God has remembered his people and vindicated his heritage; and for them these days, the fourteenth and fifteenth of the month of Adar, are to be days of assembly, of joy and of gladness before God, through all generations and for ever among his people Israel.'

## Colophon
In the fourth year of the reign of Ptolemy and Cleopatra, Dositheus, who affirmed that he was a priest and Levite, and Ptolemy his son brought the foregoing letter concerning the Purim. They maintained it as being authentic, the translation having been made by Lysimachus son of Ptolemy, a member of the Jerusalem community.